WOLVERINES IN THE SKY

Michigan's Fighter Aces Of
World War I, World War II and Korea

BY ANDREW LAYTON

"Wolverines in the Sky: Michigan's Fighter Aces of World War I, World II and Korea," by Andrew Layton. ISBN 1-58939-682-0.

Published 2005 by Virtualbookworm.com Publishing Inc., P.O. Box 9949, College Station, TX 77842, US. © 2005, Andrew Layton. All rights reserved. No part of this publication may be reproduced, stored in a retrieval system, or transmitted in any form or by any means, electronic, mechanical, recording or otherwise, without the prior written permission of Andrew Layton.

Manufactured in the United States of America.

TABLE OF CONTENTS

Acknowledgements 5
Preface.. 6
Introduction 8
World War I: 1914-1918 17
    D'Arcy F. Hilton 18
    Edward R. Grange 20
    Kenneth L. Porter.. 22
World War II: 1939-1945 24
    Walker M. Mahurin 25
    Ira C. "Ike" Kepford 28
    Phillip C. DeLong.. 30
    James F. Rigg 32
    Ernest C. Fiebelkorn 34
    Judge E. Wolfe 37
    William E. Bryan, Jr.. 39
    Carl C. Foster... 41
    Claude W. Plant, Jr... 43
    Mayo A. Hadden, Jr. 45
    George P. Novotny 47
    Charles E. Weaver 49
    James M. Morris 51
    John D. Lombard.. 53
    John E. Purdy 55
    Gerald E. Tyler 58
    Edward T. Waters 60
    John M. Wesolowski 62
    Merl W. Davenport 64
    Arthur R. Conant 65
    Urban L. Drew 67
    Charles E. Edinger 69
    Leland A. Larson 71
    James D. Mugavero... 73
    Zenneth A. Pond.. 75

Herman W. Visscher 77
Robert E. Welch 79
Murray Winfield 81
Walter J. Koraleski 82
William L. Hood, Jr. 84
John B. Mass, Jr. 85
Michael G. H. McPharlin 87
Donovan F. Smith 89
Walter A. Wood 91
Melvin M. Pritchard 92
Frank B. Baldwin 94
Raymond M. Bank 96
Robert M. Barkey 98
William A. Carlton 100
Richard E. Duffy 102
John W. Fair 104
Robert D. Gibb 106
Myron M. Hnatio 107
David P. Phillips III 109
Andrew J. Ritchey 110
Gerald L. Rounds 111
Michael T. Russo 113
Peter J. Van Der Linden, Jr. 116
Lee V. Wiseman 118
Michael R. Yunck 119
The Korean War: 1950-1953 121
Cecil G. Foster 122
Winton W. "Bones" Marshall 124
Iven C. Kincheloe, Jr. 126
Epilogue 129
Appendix 130
Bibliography 132
About the Author 134

ACKNOWLEDGEMENTS

I would like to extend thanks to a number of individuals who helped and encouraged me in the preparation of this work. Among those is Mr. Stan Bozich, curator of Michigan's Own Military and Space Museum in Frankenmuth, who provided many helpful resources and a great deal of encouragement along the way. Also thanks to my parents, Joe and Amy Layton for their support and assistance in proof reading, and to my brother Daniel for his valuable input and advise. Last but certainly not least, I owe a big thank you to the Lord for his daily guidance and inspiration, and for giving me the great opportunity to record these stories. To all of those mentioned above and also to the others not mentioned, I express my deepest gratitude.

PREFACE
What is a Fighter Ace?

FIGHTER ACE. Perhaps no other title stirs up so many thoughts of glory, adventure, and bravery as this one. But what exactly does this title mean and how many people have actually earned it? Officially, any pilot who was credited with shooting down five or more enemy aircraft in flight is eligible to be referred to as an ace. Amazingly, less than 1,500 men have achieved this incredible feat since the first dogfights took place in World War I.

To be a fighter ace, a unique combination of skills and traits were necessary. Quick reflexes often meant the difference between life and death in the sky, and keen eyesight has always been a must. In order to be a successful fighter pilot, especially in the early days of aviation, you had to be in absolutely perfect physical condition to be able to endure the incredible g-forces experienced in air combat. But the key to becoming an ace was not something to be seen on the outside. No, it was all in your head. This key was the will to succeed; the will to overcome the enemy no matter what it took, and to always come out on top.

Hollywood and the media have together portrayed fighter aces as rough, often arrogant, hard-drinking individuals who flew and lived recklessly, and wanted only to add to their own personal glory. In reality, nothing could be farther from the truth. There are exceptions to this, but for the most part, aces were just ordinary people who went to extraordinary measures to get the job done.

Whether flying over the fields of Europe, the spanning waters of the Pacific, or the jungles of China, Korea, or Vietnam, all displayed extraordinary heroism in battle, and are deserving of great respect and admiration.

It is people like them, who when called upon to defend our nation from the threat of Nazism, Japanese Imperialism, and Communism, gave all they could to ensure that victory would be won. All gave years of their lives to the war effort by serving in the military. Some gave their blood, and still suffer from the effects of wounds received in battle. And still some, at a very young age, gave their lives; the ultimate sacrifice one can give. They are the true heroes- those who did not make it back. It is to people like these, not just fighter aces, but all men and women who have served in our country's military, that we owe our freedom.

I have chosen to tell the stories of a few of these men, all natives of Michigan, who distinguished themselves in the air during a time of war. I have gotten to know many of them while working on this project, and I have greatly enjoyed hearing their stories firsthand. It is my goal to record these accounts of history so that others may have the opportunity to be as inspired by them as I was.

Andrew Layton

INTRODUCTION
The History of the Fighter Ace

IN ORDER TO BE CALLED A FIGHTER ACE, one is required to shoot down five enemy aircraft in aerial combat. As simple as it sounds, this is probably the most difficult title for a member of the armed forces to earn. So difficult in fact, that the number of American four – star generals and admirals outnumbers that of fighter aces. Only 1,432 men have ever achieved this feat, and even fewer have actually survived combat to tell about it. Of this handful of aviators, a remarkable 56 of them hail from within the borders of the state of Michigan.

Many people do not realize that the concept of military aviation dates back to the Civil War, when Professor Thaddeus Lowe devised a balloon suitable for observation over enemy lines. Lowe offered his services to the Union cause, and from his aerial perch, he observed Confederate troop positions in many of the major battles between the North and South. His finest hour came in 1862, when during the Seven Days Campaign in Eastern Virginia, he was credited with saving the Union army from almost sure defeat by spotting a large body of Confederate troops forming a surprise attack on the Union flank. As a result of this and other actions, Lowe was able to effectively demonstrate that aerial operations would change the way wars would be fought, and he was proven to be correct during the First World War.

Aircraft were first used in combat over the trenches of Europe in 1914. The world was involved in its first global conflict, and nations became embattled in fierce competition to see who could build the largest air force. Though first used strictly as instruments of observation, the importance of military aircraft had been recognized, and was well on its way to changing the world.

Observation pilots in World War I were a different kind of soldier. If they encountered an enemy aircraft while on a mission, most would wave and continue on with their duties. Pilots of both sides felt a special bond with others who shared their occupation, and at first, they simply could not bring themselves to shoot at one of their "brothers." But these feelings of goodwill would not last long, for at some point during World War I, observation planes began carrying bombs, grenades and machine guns. Though first intended to inflict damage on enemy ground positions, it was only a matter of time before aircraft fought against each other in the skies too.

The first country to name its top pilots "aces" was France. The French Flying Corps bestowed this title on all of its pilots who destroyed 10 or more German aircraft in air combat. The title referred to the highest ranking card in a playing deck. It is said that early in the war, one of the first French aces was forced to make a crash landing at a British airfield. After the Frenchman climbed out of his wrecked aircraft, he began talking with the British pilots, and showed them his impressive collection of medals. After taking a look at his high honors, one of the Brits asked how he got them, and the

Frenchman proudly announced that he was an "ace." The Englishmen had never heard of such a thing, and at first thought this strange title was a bunch of nonsense. The French aviator suddenly became very humbled when he learned that most of the British pilots had shot down many more planes than he had. For weeks after the French aviator's departure, the British jokingly kidded each other about being "aces."

Whether this story is true or not, it is a known fact that in 1917, the French and British Air Forces set the standard of ace at ten aircraft confirmed destroyed in air combat. When America joined the war effort later in that year, many of the U.S.'s high – ranking officials believed that the war would be over before any American pilot had the opportunity to shoot down so many planes. It was then decided to lower the requirements of an ace to five enemy aircraft shot down. To boost morale, many of the other allied nations quickly followed.

By the time Germany surrendered on November 11, 1918. America had produced 138 fighter aces. Leading this group with 26 kills was Captain Eddie Rickenbacker. A recipient of the Medal of Honor, Rickenbacker became known across America as the "Ace of Aces." Others to earn high honors as fighter aces were Frank Luke with 19 victories, and Raul Lufbery, who recorded 16 kills. It seemed that the American public could not get enough of this new kind of hero, and throughout the 1920's and 30's, one could find books, magazines, and even movies everywhere based on the experiences of fighter aces. Most, however, displayed him as the rough, flamboyant type that has been portrayed so often ever since.

World War II brought dramatic changes to the nature of warfare. Technologically, the planes that were being flown by the world's air forces in 1941 were the stuff of science fiction compared to the rickety old biplanes put to use during the First World War. With a new war to be fought, new heroes were needed for the public to admire. The fighter ace more than met that need. The first

American ace of the Second World War was William R. Dunn, who while serving with England's Royal Air Force in Europe, shot down his fifth German aircraft in August of 1941. The first fighter pilot to "make ace" while serving with the U.S. military was a quiet man by the name of Boyd D. Wagner. Known to all as "Buzz," Wagner flew his first combat missions in the Philippines in December of 1941. He had a remarkable talent for flying an airplane, and he put it to good use early on. In his first engagement with enemy aircraft, he downed three Japanese fighters while flying a P-40, and several days later added two more to his record, becoming the first American ace against the Japanese. The date was December 16, 1941, and the "ace race" was on.

During the course of World War II, 1,252 men earned the coveted title of ace. They become house hold names, and for a time everyone knew of the exploits of aces like Dick Bong, the top American ace of all time with 40 kills to his credit, Francis "Gabby" Gabreski, who destroyed 34 ½ planes in air combat during World War II and Korea, and the amazing Joe Foss, a larger-than-life figure who claimed a remarkable 26 planes shot out of the sky in a little over a month. Other well – known Aces of this era were Alex Vraciu who scored 19 victories while flying off the decks of U.S. Navy carriers, and Robert L. Scott with 22 planes shot down. Then there was Chuck Yeager, who claimed 13 ½ German aircraft destroyed, and the colorful David "Tex" Hill who scored 18 ¼ victories over the Japanese in China. These men, and others, now all but forgotten, fought, and some died for our freedom in far – off lands. They put their lives on the line on a daily basis for America, and made huge contributions to the defeat of the Axis powers.

One of the interesting aspects of World War II air combat is the process used to credit enemy planes destroyed. Throughout history, the words "kill," "victory," and "enemy aircraft destroyed" have been used interchangeably. In the First World War, if more than one pilot played a role in the destruction of an enemy aircraft, a whole "kill" was awarded. This, however, greatly distorted the total amount of aircraft destroyed, and caused considerable confusion in the record keeping process. Early in World War II, it was decided to award partial credit to pilots, who along with others, contributed in the destruction of an enemy airplane. This did make for some very unusual tallies however. For instance, Ray Wetmore of the 359th Fighter Group destroyed 22.56 Nazi aircraft, and Robert T. Smith of the American Volunteer Group claimed 8.9 Japanese planes destroyed.

Getting credit for an enemy aircraft kill was not as easy as it sounds. To be officially recognized with an aerial victory, at least one of the following must have occurred:

1. The enemy plane must have crashed into the ground.
2. The enemy pilot must have bailed out.
3. The enemy aircraft must have been enveloped in fire.
4. The enemy aircraft must have lost structural parts, such as a wing or tail section.

All claims had to be backed up with gun camera footage or be confirmed by a witness other than the pilot making the claim. If the criteria for a confirmed victory were not met, a claim could be classified as a "probable" victory. If hits were observed with no apparent effect, the action could then be recorded as a "damaged." The record for the most enemy aircraft destroyed in one day by an American was set by Cdr. Dave McCampbell of the U.S.

Navy, who shot down nine confirmed Japanese aircraft on October 24, 1944. McCampbell, who was awarded the Medal of Honor for his actions on this mission, finished the war as the Navy's top Ace with 34 confirmed kills.

Another confusing matter as far as tally records go is the destruction of aircraft on the ground. In the 8th, 9th and 14th Air Forces, little or no distinction was made between aircraft strafed on the ground, or aircraft blown out of the sky. The idea was to boost morale by making it easier to become an ace. Pilots such as Jim Goodson of the 4th Fighter Group, and the 368th Fighter Group's Paul Douglas, one of the most prolific strafers in history, racked up incredible amounts of aircraft destroyed on the ground. Combined with air victories, this made for some very impressive scores. The United States Navy and Marine Corps on the other hand, kept with the tradition and counted only victories over planes destroyed in air combat. With the formation of the American Fighter Aces Association in 1960, an official list of all fighter pilots credited with five or more kills in air combat was compiled, clearing up any question of eligibility based on planes destroyed on the ground. The AFAA also corrected the errors made during World War I as far as shared victories go, which dramatically reduced the scores of such pilots as Eddie Rickenbacker, who is now recognized with 24.33 kills. The top 10 American scores based on air victories alone follow:

1. Richard I. Bong, 40 kills, WWII
2. Thomas B. McGuire, 38 kills, WWII
3. Francis S. Gabreski, 34.5 kills, WWII and Korea
4. David S. McCampbell, 34 kills, WWII
5. Robert S. Johnson, 28 Kills, WWII
6. Charles H. MacDonald, 27 kills, WWII
7. George E. Preddy, 26.83 kills, WWII
8. Joseph J. Foss, 26 kills, WWII
9. John C. Meyer, 26 kills, WWII and Korea
10. Robert M. Hanson, 25 kills, WWII

Many of the great World War II fighter aces added to their combat experience during the Korean War. Seven men earned the distinction of becoming fighter aces in two wars. In all, the Korean War saw 40 individuals shoot down their fifth enemy aircraft. All but one scored their kills in the F-86 Sabre. This exception was Lt. Guy P. Bordelon of the U.S. Navy, who in a Corsair became America's last pilot to make ace while flying a propeller-driven aircraft. Leading the way for Korean War scoring was Joseph McConnell who claimed destruction of 16 MiG fighters during the course of the war. Second was James Jabara, history's first Jet Ace with 15 kills. Jabara also shot down 1 ½ aircraft during World War II for a combined total of 16 ½ confirmed victories. Manuel "Pete" Fernandez rounded out the top three with 14 ½ victories. Michigan's top ace of the conflict was Cecil G. Foster, a native of Midland, with nine confirmed kills over communist fighters.

The next, and last war to produce fighter aces was the Vietnam War. A new kind of conflict saw a new generation of fighter pilots rise to defend our nation. The first Ace of the war in Vietnam was Randy "Duke" Cunningham of the US Navy, with five kills. His Radar

Intercept Officer, Willie Driscoll, was also credited with five victories by the U.S. Navy. Others to shoot down five North Vietnamese fighters were Steve Ritchie of the U.S. Air Force, and Jeff Feinstine, an F-4 Weapon System Officer who flew for three different pilots during the course of the war. The top ace of the conflict was Ritchie's back seater, Chuck DeBellvue, who was credited with six confirmed victories. DeBellvue scored these kills while serving as Weapons System Officer for two different pilots in the 432nd Tactical Fighter Reconnaissance Wing.

Though DeBellvue, Feinstine, and Driscoll were all recognized as aces by their respective services, their names are not found on the American Fighter Aces Association's roster, because by definition, one must be the qualified pilot of an aircraft in order to gain ace status. Historians and scholars alike will argue for hours as to whether the three "back seat" aces are in fact eligible for the fighter ace title. Therefore, it is unlikely that this controversy will be put to rest any time soon.

One additional pilot, Robin Olds, who was an experienced 13 kill Fighter ace in World War II, added at least four MiG victories to his record in Vietnam. It is possible, though unconfirmed, that he is in fact the sixth ace of the Vietnam War with five victories.

Today, the number of living fighter aces is steadily decreasing. Those who are still with us live peacefully in retirement, some making occasional appearances at air shows or aviation museums. Considering the direction in which modern warfare is headed, it is unlikely that there will ever be another fighter ace. They are a thing of the past, a piece of history that must never be forgotten. So now, let's meet some of Michigan's *Wolverines in the Sky*.

WORLD WAR I
1914-1918

D'ARCY F. HILTON
8 victories
Detroit

AS MICHIGAN'S TOP WORLD WAR I ACE, D'Arcy Fowlis Hilton's life was one filled with adventure, heroism, and mystery. Though he was born on October 17, 1889 in Toronto, Canada, Hilton always considered himself a native of Detroit, the town in which he spent most of his childhood. As a young man, Hilton disagreed with the United States Government's neutral status in the growing war in Europe. As a result, he decided to get into the war himself, and at the age of 27, sailed from New York harbor in November of 1916. His destination would be Great Britain, where he hoped to become a fighter pilot.

After enlisting in England's Royal Flying Corps, Hilton received his designation as a pilot in the spring of 1917, and was assigned to the 29th Royal Flying Corps Squadron, operating out of France. Having checked out in Nieuport 17 "Scout" aircraft, he quickly gained a reputation as a very talented pilot. Hilton scored his first two kills, a German balloon and an Albatros DV aircraft on July 31, 1917. On August 9, his patrol engaged eight enemy aircraft, of which Hilton claimed one destroyed. Obviously on a hot streak, he bagged another Albatros DV just two days later, bringing his tally to four. Within a week, Hilton had his fifth and sixth kills under his belt, making him the only American pilot serving with the Royal Flying Corps to "make ace" in the Nieuport 17.

Though he was now a full –fledged fighter ace, Hilton didn't score again until October 30th, when he emptied a full barrel of ammunition on a two-seat observation plane over France. This aircraft was confirmed on Hilton's record, as it was seen to spin wildly out of control before it crashed. By the end of 1917, Hilton had destroyed one more Albatross DV to bring his final score of destroyed enemy aircraft to eight. For his overall heroism in combat, he was awarded the British Military Cross.

As the war in Europe drew to a close, Hilton was ordered back to England where he became a flight instructor at Deseranto Field. While serving in this capacity, he was again decorated for his service, this time with the British Air Force Cross. Hilton eventually separated from the Royal Flying Corps, and returned to his birthplace of Toronto. Unfortunately, Hilton's post-war life and his image as a hero of the First World War were constantly marred by financial problems and bad publicity. Hilton finally slipped into obscurity in the mid 1920's following a divorce and passed away in October of 1973. His son, following in the footsteps of his father, also became a fighter pilot and was killed due to unfortunate circumstances in World War II.

EDWARD R. GRANGE
5 victories
Lansing

LANSING, MICHIGAN was the birthplace of the Wolverine State's first ace on January 11, 1892. In 1916, Edward R. Grange traveled to Great Britain to join the Royal Naval Air Service. After receiving his flight training in Canada, Grange was assigned to the First Naval Wing, and began logging combat missions in the Sopwith Pup aircraft.

Grange managed to score his first aerial victory on September 25, 1916, before being transferred to the Eighth Naval Squadron in October of that year. On January 4, 1917, Grange participated in a harrowing air battle in which he shot down three German Albatros D.II's. Each of his kills that day were seen to crash somewhere north of Bapaume, France.

Now having shot down four enemy aircraft, Grange did not have to wait long to become an ace. Just three days later, he again encountered an Abatros D.II and shot it down in flames. He then spotted two more enemy aircraft hotly pursuing one of his squadron mates. Grange maneuvered his Sopwith in an attempt to rescue his fellow pilot, but didn't see a third Albatros coming in behind him. He tried to turn away, but it was too late, and there was nothing he could do. The German pilot fired, badly damaging Grange's plane. The American, though seriously injured in the shoulder, somehow kept control of his crippled aircraft, and later landed at a nearby friendly airfield. Grange, suffering badly from his wounds, was soon shipped back to England where he recovered and later served as a flight instructor.

After being released from military service at the end of World War One, Grange settled in Canada where he became a successful businessman and engineer. He again offered his service to the Allies during World War Two, serving in the Royal Canadian Air Force as an inspector and auditor. A recipient of the British Distinguished Service Cross and the French Croix de Guerre, Grange passed away on July 13, 1988 at his home in Toronto, Canada.

KENNETH L. PORTER
5 victories
Dowagiac

KENNETH LEE PORTER was born on the 6th of December, 1896 in Dowagiac, Michigan. As a young man, He attended the University of Michigan, where he received a degree in engineering before enlisting in the United States Army Air Service on August 6, 1917. After extensive training in both Canada and Texas, Porter received his silver aviator's wings and the gold bars of a second lieutenant on January 16, 1918. He was destined for France and the 147th Aero Squadron where he would fly the Nieuport 28 aircraft in combat against the Germans.

Ken began logging combat missions with his unit, but did not score his first kill until July 2, 1918, when he and four other Americans encountered twelve Pfalz D.III aircraft over Chateau Thierry, France. As soon as the enemy planes were sighted, Porter maneuvered his Nieuport to get between them and the sun. Along with his fellow Americans, Porter gained the advantage, but not without great difficulty. While three of the other Americans engaged the lower six German aircraft, Porter, along with one other pilot, attacked the upper formation. In a bold maneuver, Ken caught one of the Pflaz's and sent him spinning to earth in a ball of flame, resulting in a confirmed kill for the young Lieutenant. For his actions on this day, Lt. Porter received the Distinguished Service Cross, a decoration second only in precedence to the Medal of Honor.

In August of 1918, the 147th Aero Squadron traded in their obsolete Nieuports for new SPAD S.XIII aircraft. This was the plane that Ken was to enjoy his greatest successes in, for on October 12, 1918, Porter shot down his fifth enemy aircraft to become an ace. Porter, who had become a flight commander just two days earlier, could now count on his personal record two fighters and three bombers destroyed. His scoring would end there though, as the war ended less than a month later. After Germany's surrender on November 18, 1918, Ken returned to the United States, and was released from military service on February 26, 1919. By the time of his discharge, he had added to his list of decorations the Silver Star and the French Croix de Guerre with palm.

In the post-war years, Ken resumed his career as an engineer, working at the Burroughs Business Machine Company and later at the Pesco Pump Company in New York. During World War II, he was employed by the Boeing Corporation where he worked on various war-related projects. Later in life, Porter moved to Jackson Heights, New York, staying active in the American Fighting Pilot's Association. He passed away on February 3, 1988, and is buried at Arlington National Cemetery in Virginia.

WORLD WAR II
1939-1945

WALKER M. MAHURIN
24.5 victories
Benton Harbor

AS MICHIGAN'S "ACE OF ACES" and the only ace to down aircraft in the European and Pacific theaters that also scored kills during the Korean War, Walker Melville Mahurin was born in Benton Harbor, Michigan on December 5, 1918. He lived in Ann Arbor for the first year of his life, but was then adopted by a family from Fort Wayne, Indiana; the place where he would spend the rest of his childhood. Mahurin enlisted in the Army Air Corps on September 29, 1941, and after graduating from flight school, was assigned to the 56th Fighter Group based in England. He scored his first aerial victories on August 17, 1943, when he shot down two German FW-190 fighters on a bomber escort mission over Regensburg, Germany. He claimed two more destroyed on September 9, and gained ace status on October 4, 1943 with the destruction of three ME-110 twin engine fighters. Mahurin knocked down three more ME-110's on November 26th to become the first American pilot in the European Theater to score 10 aerial kills, and the first to receive the Silver Star for heroism.

During the winter of 1943-1944 Mahurin's tally of kills rose rapidly. On March 27, 1944, six days after his promotion to Major, Mahurin shared credit for destruction of a DO-217 bomber for his 20th kill, but moments later was shot down himself. He bailed out of his stricken P-47 and with the aid of French resistance forces, was able to evade capture for two months and eventually make his way back to England. When he returned to his unit, Mahurin learned that Air Force policies had grounded him because of his knowledge of the French underground forces. Mahurin returned home to the US, and after several moths of stateside duty, was returned to combat as commander of the 3rd Air Commando Squadron operating in the Southwest Pacific area. Flying P-51 *Mustangs,* Mahurin engaged in aerial operations from Okinawa to New Guinea, achieving his final air-to-air kill of World War II on January 14, 1945 with the destruction of a Japanese Mitsubishi Ki-46 "Dinah" reconnaissance aircraft. Mahurin was eventually shot down again by ground fire, and after spending hours floating in a life raft, was rescued by American forces. Upon completion of his second combat tour, Mahurin returned to the United States and was promoted to Lieutenant Colonel on May 28, 1945.

As the Korean War broke out in June of 1950, Mahurin was offered an opportunity to escape from a desk job at the Pentagon and fly combat missions in Korea. Mahurin jumped at the offer, and was soon flying F-86 *Sabres* with the 51st Fighter Interceptor Wing from Suwan Airfield, South Korea. By 1952, Mahurin had destroyed 3.5 North Korean MiG -15 fighters, and had flown dozens of combat missions over enemy territory. Transferred to the 4th Fighter Wing on March 18, 1952, Mahurin soon assumed command of the unit. He flew with this organization until May 13th of that year, when he was shot down again by ground fire. Mahurin crash landed his burning F-86, but was captured by North Korean forces.

Throughout his 16 month captivity, Mahurin endured unbelievable hardships and almost daily torture. His captors placed him in solitary confinement, and subjected him to brainwashing. They continually questioned him on concepts of "germ warfare," claiming falsely that America had been using such inhumane methods of warfare against the North Koreans for years. Mahurin feared he would give in to the communist's demands, and attempted to commit suicide. Caught in the act, Mahurin survived, and eventually devised a false confession, stating that he had dropped several canisters filled with insects over North Korean lines. This confession was so full of inaccuracies that it caused the North Koreans, who then began treating their prisoners somewhat better, a great deal of confusion. Unknown to Mahurin was that the war had already been over for months.

Bud was finally released from captivity in September, 1953, and received orders promoting him to full Colonel. His willingness to relate his experiences as a prisoner of war and the methods of brainwashing and torture used by enemy nations served as a great aid in the development of the U.S. survival training courses. In 1956, Mahurin left the Air Force after more than 16 years of service to our nation to take a senior position in the aircraft industry.

Throughout his illustrious career, Walker M. Mahurin received numerous awards and decorations from around the world, including the Distinguished Service Cross, the Silver Star, the Distinguished Flying Cross with 6 oak leaf clusters, the Purple Heart, the Air Medal with 6 oak leaf clusters, the British Distinguished Flying Cross, the French Croix de Guerre, and the Belgian Croix de Guerre. Now living in Newport Beach, California with his wife, Jo, Mahurin is still a very active public speaker and pilot, even as he goes into his eighties.

IRA C. "IKE" KEPFORD
17 victories
Muskegon

BORN IRA CASSIUS KEPFORD on May 29, 1919 in Harvey, Illinois, "Ike" Kepford moved to Muskegon, Michigan with his family at the age of eight. Kepford began his military career in 1941, when he enlisted in the U.S. Naval Reserves. He earned his wings of gold in Corpus Christi, Texas on November 5, 1942, before being assigned to VF-17, which was equipped with F4U *Corsairs*. Kepford arrived in the Pacific Theater in October, 1943 and flew his first mission on November 11 of that year. It was on this day that he and other pilots of VF-17 were tasked with flying cover for the aircraft carrier U.S.S. *Bunker Hill*. One of the eight American pilots involved in this mission spotted a formation of over 100 Japanese aircraft; "Zeroes," "Kates," and "Vals," preparing to make a bombing run on the *Bunker Hill*. Tearing into the enemy formation, Ike downed one of them only 1,000 yards from the ship. Seconds later, three more enemy planes fell to his guns in quick succession after Kepford saw them trying to make an escape from the massacre. The intense anti aircraft fire, along with the Corsairs of the Jolly Rogers soon broke up the attack, saving the Bunker Hill from almost certain destruction.

As the Corsairs of VF-17 began to reform after the action, Ike spotted a lone Val dive bomber on the horizon. He jumped the single aircraft and fired a few shots from his six .50 caliber machine guns before realizing that he was out of ammunition. Kepford, by now almost out of fuel, sent a radio transmission to the Bunker Hill requesting permission to land on the carrier. The sailors of the Bunker Hill gladly took him aboard, happy to assist one of their flying defenders. After enjoying a cup of coffee with the Bunker Hill's Captain, Kepford took off in his refueled and rearmed Corsair, heading in the direction of the Jolly Rogers's home base, an airfield located on New Georgia Island.

Kepford began one of the greatest scoring sprees of any American pilot in history when he flamed two Zero fighters on January 27, 1944 to make ace. He claimed four more destroyed on the 29th, one on February 3rd, and three on February 19. By the time he returned to the United States after completing his tour of duty in March of 1944, Kepford had been credited with 17 confirmed victories, one probable, and one damaged. He was known as the top Navy Ace in history, and held that distinction for over three months. Ike's pair of Navy Crosses, his Silver Star, three Distinguished Flying Crosses, and Air Medal made him one of the most highly decorated naval aviators of all time, and a world renowned hero.

Kepford retired from the Navy on June 1, 1956 with the rank of Lieutenant Commander, and soon afterwards began working for Rexall Drug Stores, eventually becoming president of the company's eastern division. America lost a great hero on January 19, 1987 when he died at his home near Traverse City, Michigan.

PHILLIP C. DELONG
13.17 victories
Jackson

PHILLIP CUNIFFE DELONG was born on July 9, 1919 in Jackson, Michigan. He attended the University of Omaha before entering the Naval Aviation Cadet Program, which he graduated from on December 16, 1942 in Corpus Christi, Texas. Assigned to Marine Fighting Squadron 212, flying F4U Corsairs in the South Pacific, DeLong was credited with his first two kills in January, 1944, when he flamed two Zeroes and damaged a third over Kabanga Bay. Eight days later, he claimed another pair of Zeroes in a dogfight over Blanche Bay, and bagged two more Zeroes plus one shared kill on January 23 over the course of two missions that he flew that day. Before the month was out, DeLong had destroyed two more Japanese aircraft, including a Zero on the 29th , and a "Hamp" fighter on the 31st. DeLong rounded out his World War II scoring with three "Val" Dive bombers splashed near Green Island on February 15.

With 11.17 Japanese aircraft to his credit, DeLong was rotated home for an assignment as Flight Instructor at Cherry Point, North Carolina, where he served until the end of the war. He again saw combat during the Korean War, once again flying Corsairs from the decks of the carrier *USS Bataan*. DeLong received credit for two communist Yak-9 fighters destroyed on April 21, 1951, therefore joining a very select group of aviators who have downed multiple enemy aircraft in two wars.

During the remainder of his career, Delong commanded a number Marine fighter squadrons, and served as commander of the Marine Corps Air Facility on Okinawa before his retirement as full Colonel in 1969. During his 27 years of service, DeLong received the Silver Star, the Legion of Merit, the Distinguished Flying Cross with 6 Gold Stars, the Air Medal with 16 Gold Stars, and the Navy/Marine Corps Commendation Medal. Today, DeLong makes his home on Treasure Island, Florida.

JAMES F. RIGG
11 victories
Saginaw

JAMES FRANCIS RIGG was born on July 18, 1915 in Saginaw, Michigan. He attended the University of Michigan before entering the U.S. Naval Air Service on July 7, 1937. After completing his training as a fighter pilot, Jim was assigned briefly to VF-2, and was later transferred to VF-7 in June of 1939. He also spent time flying F2F's from the decks of the U.S.S. *Wasp* with VF-72. As World War II broke out, Rigg found himself assigned as a flight instructor, and served in this capacity until September of 1942, and then spent eleven months on the U.S.S. *Wolverine*. Rigg's first combat assignment came with VF-15, which he joined as executive officer. Outfitted with the new F6F *Hellcat*, VF-15 was assigned to the U.S.S. *Essex*, and was destined to become the greatest U.S. Navy Fighting Squadron in history. Rigg became commander of this distinguished unit on March 1, 1944 when he was promoted to Lieutenant Commander. He achieved his first confirmed victories on June 11, 1944 with the destruction of a Mitsubishi A6M5 "Zeke" and a Kawasaki Ki-61 "Tony." He again tasted success eight days later when he was credited with an Aichi D3A "Val" destroyed, and an additional four "Vals" and a "Zeke" probably destroyed. On September 10, 1944, Lt. Commander Rigg shot down a Mitsubishi Ki-46 "Dinah" over Mindanao in the Philippines, but his greatest day in combat came two days later on September 12, 1944. While leading an early morning sweep over a Japanese airfield, Rigg shot down a Nakajima Ki-44 "Tojo" just as it was taking off from the runway. He swung the nose of his Hellcat back around to face three *Zekes* who had been scrambled to defend the airstrip. No match for the mighty Hellcat and its ace pilot, Rigg had all three enemy aircraft spinning to the ground in flames within seconds. Soon after finishing off the last of these three, another *Zeke* caught his eye. Rigg engaged this Japanese pilot, and in a nerve-racking dogfight chased the *Zeke* through the treetops, and finally shot him down over the water for his fifth kill of the day. Not only had Rigg become an ace, but he had become a rare "ace in a day."

Rigg's next successes came one month later on October 12 when his formations of F6F's were jumped by a large number of *Zekes* over Formosa. Rigg climbed to meet their challenge, and quickly shot down one of the attackers. He also scored hits on four other Japanese fighters that day, receiving damaged credit for each of them.
Rigg's last victory came on November 11, 1944 in the form of a Nakajima Ki-43 "Oscar." This kill would bring Rigg's final score to 11 confirmed, 5 probable, and 5 damaged.

Remaining in the Navy after the war, Rigg served as skipper of VC-12 from July 1953 to August 1954, and was then executive officer of the U.S.S. Tarawa from November 1955 to February 1957. He was promoted to Captain on July 1, 1957 before retiring on July 1, 1963 to go into the book binding business. During Captain Rigg's 27 years in the U.S. Navy, he received numerous decorations and awards including the Navy
Cross, 7 Distinguished Flying Crosses, a Bronze Star, and 10 Air Medals. He now makes his home in East Greenwich, Rhode Island.

ERNEST C. FIEBELKORN
9.5 victories
Lake Orion

ERNEST CHARLES FIEBELKORN, a native of Lake Orion, was born on December 12, 1922. He attended Michigan State University before enlisting in the U.S. Army Air Force in 1943. "Fieb," as he was called, graduated from flight school at Williams Army Air Force Base, Arizona, even though he had a tough time getting his six-foot, four-inch, 225-pound frame into the tiny cockpits of the Army fighters. Still, he was assigned to the 20th Fighter Group, flying P-51 Mustangs on the 11th of January, 1944. Fieb started his tour of duty in Europe rather slowly, and did not receive credit for his first confirmed kill until September 28, when he destroyed three ME-109 fighters, along with an FW-190 over Magdeburg, Germany, earning himself a Silver Star. Fiebelkorn's next successes came on November 2nd, 1944, when three Nazi fighters fell to his guns over Leipzing. His P-51, named "June Nite" after his wife, now wore seven swastikas painted under the cockpit, each representing a victory over an enemy aircraft. Fiebelkorn achieved what was perhaps his greatest feat only five days later when he shared destruction of an ME-262 jet. Shooting down a jet fighter was a great accomplishment in itself, but this kill was even more prestigious because the pilot of the German craft was Major Walter Nowotny, the fifth-ranking Luftwaffe Ace of all time with 258 allied aircraft to his credit.

While Fiebelkorn was racking up his impressive combat record, he was also gaining a reputation as one of the funniest and best-liked pilots in the 20th Fighter Group. One of Fieb's fellow pilots remembered how on October 2, 1944, Maj. Glenn Miller and the Army Air Force Band visited the 20th Fighter Group's Kingscliffe, England airfield. While Miller was thrilling the audience with the big-band sounds of his orchestra, Fieb decided to give them a little more excitement. He brought his Mustang in low, and flew it right through the hanger that the concert was being held in...upside-down! Fieb was then grounded, not surprisingly. He somehow managed to get into combat again, however, and added two more German aircraft to his record by the end of the war. His final tally would stand at 9 ½ confirmed aerial victories, 1 damaged, and 2 destroyed on the ground.

Fiebelkorn would also see combat in Korea, where he gained the unfortunate distinction of being the first U.S. Airman killed in that conflict. As the story goes, Fieb had volunteered to participate in a mission to rescue an infantry unit that had been trapped by enemy fire. The date was July 6, 1950, and Fieb, who found the weather in the area to be bad, broke off from the rest of the American formation and dove down to support the infantry column alone. It was only a matter of time before he lost control of his F-82 Twin Mustang and crashed. Feibelkorn's remains, along with the body of his radar observer, John J. Higgins, were not recovered for over 2 ½ years. After they were found on a mountain 40 miles north of Seoul, they were both interned at the Arlington National Cemetery in Washington, D.C. Fiebelkorn's memory is preserved today with a display highlighting the events of his career at Michigan's Own Inc. Museum in Frankenmuth, Michigan. Among the items on display are his two Silver Stars, two Distinguished Flying Crosses, Purple Heart, and six Air Medals.

JUDGE E. WOLFE
9 victories
Flint

JUDGE EDMOND WOLFE was born on July 27, 1916 in a family-built house near Flint, Michigan. He attended Coshocton High School and later graduated from the Miami University of Ohio in 1937 before going to work as an accountant at General Motors. Judge enlisted in the Army Air Corps in 1941 and received his commission and rating as a pilot in June 1942. Soon afterwards, he was assigned to the 318th Fighter Group flying the P-47 *Thunderbolt* and was shipped to the Pacific Theater. Wolfe's first aerial victories came on February 11, 1945 when he knocked down two twin-engine Japanese bombers on a mission over Iwo Jima. Wolfe's own plane was shot up in the process, which forced him to make an emergency landing at Iwo Jima.

Perhaps Wolfe's greatest claim to fame was that he was the first pilot in history to down an enemy plane by using rockets. As the story goes, Wolfe was carrying a load of air-to-ground rockets on his P-47 when his formation encountered a group of Japanese Zero fighters. Normally, a pilot would jettison his entire external ordinance before engaging in air combat in order to lighten his plane, but this option did not appeal to Wolfe. He fired four of his rockets at the first Zero that presented itself, and scored a direct hit. The force of the blast rocked his plane out of control briefly as he flew through the smoke of the burning aircraft. Wolfe later said that this was the greatest thrill he ever experienced.

Judge certainly had a knack for making spectacular kills. On another occasion, an enemy aircraft had gone into a spin to evade him. Wolfe executed a "spit-s" dive in pursuit, and while upside down caught the plane in his sights and blew it up with a short machine gun burst. As incredible as these experiences must have been, June 10, 1945 saw Wolfe fly his best mission of the war. While leading a flight of nine American aircraft, Wolfe was jumped by 60 Japanese fighters. In 10 minutes of gut-wrenching combat, the Americans downed 13 of the attackers, with Wolfe accounting for four of them. For his valor on this mission, he would later receive the Silver Star.

As the war in the Pacific drew to a close, Major Wolfe returned to the United States after completing his tour of duty. He left the Air Force for a short time to return to his position at GM, but re-enlisted in July of 1947. He was assigned to the 373rd Fighter Group based at Langley, Virginia, where he flew the F-80 *Shooting Star*. Tragically, on November 24, 1948, Wolfe was killed when the engine of his plane failed on takeoff.

Though his life was cut far too short, Judge E. Wolfe received a number of decorations for his military service, including the Distinguished Service Cross, the Silver Star, the Distinguished Flying Cross with one oak leaf cluster, and the Air Medal with one oak leaf cluster. His final tally of aircraft destroyed was 9 confirmed and 1 probably destroyed.

WILLIAM E. BRYAN, JR.
8.5 victories
Flint

WILLIAM ELMER BRYAN, JR. was born in Flint, Michigan on October 5, 1921, where he graduated from High School in 1939. He enlisted in the U.S. Army Air Corps in March, 1942 and entered aviation cadet training in June 1942. Bryan received his pilot wings and commission as second lieutenant in February, 1943.

Serving with the 339th Fighter Group in Europe, Bryan flew the P-51 *Mustang* in 114 combat missions and was credited with 8.5 enemy planes destroyed. Among his victories were two ME-109, an ME-410, and five FW-190s shot down in aerial combat.

At the end of the war in December 1945, Bryan returned to the United States. He served at Headquarters Tactical Air Command, Langley Air Force Base, Va., and then acted as an advisor to Air National Guard fighter squadrons in Minnesota and South Dakota. In August 1949 he was assigned as operations and training officer for an Air Force Reserve wing at Scott Air Force Base, Ill.

During the Korean War in August 1950, Bryan was assigned to the 18th Fighter Bomber Wing, and flew 121 combat missions, again in the P-51 Mustang. He returned from Korea in April 1951 and was assigned to Headquarters Tactical Air Command with duties involving joint air-ground tactical doctrine under the Deputy Chief of Staff for Operations. He attended the Armed Forces' Staff College, Norfolk, Va., from January 1955 to June 1955 and then was assigned to Headquarters U.S. Air Force with the Tactical Fighter Branch in the Directorate of Requirements.

From August 1959 to August 1962, General Bryan served as chief, Air Offense Division, at Headquarters U.S. Air Forces in Europe, Wiesbaden, Germany. On his return to the United States, he entered the National War College, Washington, D.C. After graduation in July 1963, he was assigned to Nellis Air Force Base, Nev., as commandant of the Air Force Fighter Weapons School and later was vice commander of the 4520th Combat Crew Training Wing.

In December 1970 General Bryan assumed duties as commander of the Nineteenth Air Force, TAC, with headquarters at Seymour Johnson Air Force Base, N.C. He was transferred to Allied Forces Central Europe headquarters in July 1972 with duties as deputy chief of staff for operations and intelligence and as senior U.S. representative to the headquarters.

He retired in 1973 as a Major General, and now lives in Mississippi with his wife Olive. During his illustrious career, Bryan received the Distinguished Service Cross, the Distinguished Service Medal, the Legion of Merit, the Distinguished Flying Cross with four oak leaf clusters, the Bronze Star Medal, and Air Medal with 23 oak leaf clusters.

CARL C. FOSTER
8.5 victories
Detroit

A NATIVE OF DETROIT, Carl Clifford Foster volunteered for service as a fighter pilot in the U.S. Navy early in World War II. Upon his completion of fighter training in the F6F *Hellcat*, Foster was assigned to VF-30, a Navy fighter squadron operating off of the decks of the USS Belleau Wood (CVL-24). He and his squadron mates were shipped to the Pacific Theater of Operations where they would soon face pilots of the Japanese Naval Air Force in aerial combat. On April 6, 1945, Lt. Foster and 13 other American aviators were scrambled to intercept an attacking formation of 47 Japanese *Kamikaze* aircraft. Within 28 minutes, all 47 enemy planes had been downed, with Foster bagging a total of six hostile aircraft. His claims for the day consisted of three *Zeke* Fighters and three *Val* Dive Bombers. It was for his incredible flying skill on this mission that Foster received the Navy Cross, America's second highest decoration for heroism. Foster's six kills in one day would not be matched by any other pilot from Michigan, and would tie him for third place overall on the list of top one-day scorers.

By the end of World War II, Carl Foster had added 2 ½ enemy planes to his official record, and had been credited with the single-handed sinking of a Japanese cargo ship. He had to his name the Navy Cross, the Distinguished Flying Cross, and six Air Medals. After his return to the United States, Foster elected to remain in the

Naval Service, and eventually retired at the rank of Commander, having served at the Grosse Isle Naval Reserve Center in his home state of Michigan. Cdr. Carl C. Foster passed away on August 15, 1988.

CLAUDE W. PLANT, JR.

8.5 victories
Grand Rapids

GRAND RAPIDS, MICHIGAN was the birthplace of Claude William Plant, Jr. on October 4, 1919. Plant, who joined the Navy's Aviation Cadet program in March 1942, received his aviator's wings on June 16, 1943 in Jacksonville, Florida. After additional training on the *USS Wolverine* stationed in the Great Lakes, Plant was assigned to VF-15 which was about to embark from Atlantic City, New Jersey on the *USS Essex* for combat in the South Pacific.

Plant flew a number of combat missions early in his combat tour without scoring against a single aerial target. His wait paid off though on June 19, 1944, when he flamed four *Zero* fighters during what would later become known the "Great Marianas Turkey Shoot." Less than a week later, Plant destroyed one Zero and shared a second with Cdr. Dave McCampbell, who would go on to be the top ace in Naval aviation history with 34 kills. Now an ace himself, Plant's next victories came on September 9, 1944 when he downed two Val dive bombers over the Philippine Islands. Just three days later, he destroyed what would be his last kill over an enemy airfield on Cebu Island. Minutes after downing the Zero, Plant was jumped by several enemy fighters who blasted his F6F *Hellcat* from dead astern. Plant bailed out of his stricken aircraft, but was captured by Japanese forces who later executed him. During Ensign Plant's brief military service he was decorated with the Silver Star, the Distinguished Flying Cross, seven Air Medals, and the Purple Heart.

MAYO A. HADDEN, JR.
8 victories
Holland

MAYO ADDISON "MIKE" HADDEN, JR. was born on August 14, 1916 in Holland, Michigan. He graduated from Hope College in 1938, and entered Navy flight training in March of 1941. He received his rating as a Naval aviator on January 22, 1942, and reported to VF-9 for combat duty in North Africa as part of operation "Torch." Hadden flew several combat missions against Vichy French forces from the decks of the *USS Ranger* in F4F *Wildcats* before he and his unit were rotated home for a period of leave.

Hadden served his second combat tour with VF-9 as well, which was now operating from the *USS Essex* in the Pacific. He scored his first aerial victory over Wake Island on October 5, 1943, but he himself was critically wounded during the mission. Not letting his injuries stop him, Hadden downed a Val dive bomber on November 11 over the Solomon Islands, and became an ace on February 17, 1944 when he destroyed three Zeroes over Eten Island. Three days later, he accounted for another trio of Zeroes between Saipan and Taiwan to bring his final tally to eight enemy aircraft destroyed.

Following Hadden's service in World War II, he served on the *USS Salamaua* from December 1945 to June 1946. He later joined VF-8 as executive officer in June 1947, and took command of VF-73 in July 1948. Hadden also commanded the *USS Graffias* from May

1963 to July 1964 before leading the *USS Hornet* until July 1965. He then spent two years as Deputy Director for Operations, Office of Political Military Affairs in the State Department. Later assignments saw him command the Icelandic Defense Force and Fleet Air Keflavik before his promotion to Rear Admiral on April 1, 1969. In November of 1970, Hadden assumed command of all air wings in the U.S. Atlantic Fleet. He retired from the military on July 1, 1973 after a full career in the service of the United States. During his career, Hadden received the Silver Star, the Legion of Merit with one Gold Star, the Distinguished Flying Cross With two Gold Stars, the Purple Heart with two Gold Stars, the Air Medal with two Gold Stars, and the Navy Commendation Medal. Admiral Hadden passed away in Cocoa Beach, Florida in December of 1986.

GEORGE P. NOVOTNY
8 victories
Allen Park

BORN ON FEBRUARY 22, 1920 in Toledo, Ohio, George Peter Novotny left his studies at DeSales College in Ohio to enlist in the Army Air Corps on January 5, 1942. Accepted for flight training, Novotny graduated from Class 43-A at Spence Field, Georgia before being assigned to Harding Field, Mississippi for additional training in the P-40 *Warhawk*. In June of 1943, he was thrust into the war over North Africa, where he served with the 317th Fighter Squadron of the 325th Fighter Group in Tunisia.

Wasting little time getting into combat, Novotny shot down an Italian MC.202 fighter and a German ME-109 on July 20. He scored again in the P-40 with the destruction of an ME-109 on August 28 before the 325th was re-equipped with P-47's in late September. On November 20, 1943, Novotny had the honor of flying escort for President Franklin D. Roosevelt's aircraft, which was en-route to the famous Tehran Conference.

Novotny's next kills came on January 30, 1944 when the 325th Fighter Group encountered a large number of German aircraft over the Villaorba area. Novotny picked off two Ju-52 transport planes and an Hs-156 to become an ace. He logged two more aerial victories, an ME-109 on March 18, 1944, and an MC.202 on April 6, before being sent back to the United States in June of 1944.

47

Novotny served as a flight instructor until he separated from the Air Corps in September of 1945 to return to college. Awarded the Distinguished Flying Cross and the Air Medal with 14 Oak Leaf Clusters, Novotny now makes his home in Allen Park, Michigan.

CHARLES E. WEAVER
8 victories
Detroit

BORN ON JULY 30, 1923 in Detroit, Charles Elon Weaver was attending Michigan State University when he applied for flight training with the U.S. Army Air Forces. He pinned on his aviator's wings and the gold bars of a second lieutenant on February 8, 1944, graduating from class 44-B at Napier Field, Alabama. After additional training in the P-40 *Warhawk*, Weaver was assigned to the 362nd Fighter Squadron, 357th Fighter Group, stationed at Leiston Field in Suffolk, England. Here Weaver would transition to P-51 *Mustangs* and participate in combat missions over occupied Europe.

Approximately one month after his arrival in England, Weaver downed his first enemy aircraft, a German ME-109 on September 19, 1944. Two FW-190's fell to his guns on November 27, and he claimed another ME-109 on December 23. Weaver's next kills came on January 14, 1945, when he shot down two German fighters on a bomber escort mission over Germany to make ace. He again scored against an ME-109 on March 24, and claimed his last aerial victory over Prauge/Ryuzyne airfield when he shot up an ME-262 jet fighter while it was landing. Weaver finished his combat tour in Europe with 73 combat missions under his belt and 8 aerial victories. He left the service in October of 1945, having been awarded the Distinguished Flying Cross with one Oak Leaf Cluster, the Air Medal with fifteen Oak

Leaf Clusters, and the French Croix de Guerre with Palm. Today, Chuck Weaver makes his home in Savannah, Georgia.

JAMES M. MORRIS
7.3 victories
Detroit

JAMES MADISON MORRIS was born on April 9, 1920 in Columbus, Ohio, but spent much of his childhood in Detroit, Michigan. He entered the United States Army Air Force in February 1942 and graduated from class 42-I at Luke Field, Arizona before being assigned to the 20th Fighter Group's 77th Fighter Squadron, which was then stationed at Kingscliffe, England in August of 1943.

Morris had his first confrontation with enemy aircraft on February 5, 1944 when he and two other 20th Fighter Group pilots shared credit for a Heinkel 111 bomber. Morris would not have to wait more than three days to claim his next victories, which came in the form of two ME-109's and two FW-190's. Morris's incredible feat of four kills on one mission set a record for American pilots in Europe that would not be broken for several months.

Jim received ace status just a few days later on February 11, when he flamed an ME-109 near Giessen, Germany. Before the month was out, his score stood at 6 1/3 enemy aircraft destroyed, his latest being an ME-110 shot down over Schweinfurt, Germany on the 24th. Morris's next kill took place on July 7, when he destroyed an ME-410 between Leipzing and Halle, Germany. Jim was shot down on this very mission, safely bailed out of his stricken craft, but was captured soon afterwards and spent the rest of the war as a prisoner of the Germans.

Jim Morris's final tally of enemy aircraft destroyed would stand at 7.3 confirmed, though he would have almost certainly gone on to be one of the top Aces in the European Theater if he had not been shot down. Morris remained in the Air Force after the war, commanding several fighter units and logging flight hours in F-80's and F-105's. In 1965, Jim requested a combat assignment in Vietnam, but developed a blood clot in his leg and was forced to return to the United States before seeing combat. After commanding a squadron of F-4's at MacDill, Air Force Base in Florida, Morris retied from the Air Force in 1969, having attained the rank of Lieutenant Colonel. He went into the insurance business as a civilian, and now lives in Tampa, Florida with his wife Eleanor.

JOHN D. LOMBARD
7 victories
Ionia

BORN ON JULY 1, 1919 in Ionia, Michigan, John Daniel Lombard graduated from Ionia High School as valedictorian of the class of 1937. Earning a bachelor of science degree in physics from Olivet College in 1940, he enlisted in the Army Air Corps as an aviation cadet soon after his graduation. Lombard won his wings as a qualified aviator on February 7, 1941 at Kelly Field, Texas, and from there was assigned to the 16th Pursuit Squadron, stationed at Hamilton Field, California.

In March of 1942, Lombard's unit was deployed to the China-Burma-India theater of operations, where it was attached to the 23rd Fighter Group stationed in Kunming, China. Operating with the P-40 *Warhawk*, the 23rd Fighter Group had been activated on July 2, 1942 to absorb a number of U.S pilots from the disbanded mercenary unit known as the American Volunteer Group. The AVG, or "Flying Tigers" as they were affectionately called by the Chinese, were a group of American trained ex-fighter pilots who were recruited by the Chinese Government to assist in the organization of China's Air Force. In a little over six months of combat, the Flying Tigers racked up a combat record that is yet to matched by any fighter group, downing at least 297 Japanese aircraft in aerial combat, with a loss of only eight American pilots. When the AVG was disbanded in July of 1942, many of its members elected to rejoin the Army Air

Force, and with the addition of many fresh pilots like John Lombard, would go on to become one of the most distinguished groups of warriors in U.S. Air Force history.

Lombard eventually proved to become one of the most distinguished men in this elite squadron, downing a Japanese fighter over Leiyang, China on July 31, 1942. He flamed another enemy plane on November 2nd, and ran his score to three just one week later in an aerial duel over Kweilin Airfield. Obviously on a hot streak, Lombard added two more kills on the 23rd and 27th of November with the destruction of a Japanese "Lily" bomber and an "Oscar" fighter respectively. He again scored on January 16, 1943 to bring his tally to six.

On June 1, 1943, Lombard assumed command of the 74th Fighter Squadron, and was promoted to the rank of Major. His seventh and final kill came on June 14, 1943 over Nanchang, China; just two weeks before he was killed in a flight accident during bad weather. During his brief military career, John Lombard was decorated with an impressive list of awards, including the Silver Star, the Distinguished Flying Cross with one Oak Leaf Cluster, the Purple Heart, The Air Medal with four Oak Leaf Clusters, and from the Chinese government, the Golden Air Hero Medal.

JOHN E. PURDY
7 victories
Wyandotte

WYANDOTTE, MICHIGAN was the birthplace of John Edgar Purdy on June 17, 1919. Jack began his military career on June 21, 1941 at the age of 22, when he was drafted for service with the U.S. Army Calvary. After completing his basic training at Fort Riley, Kansas, Purdy was sent to Fort Snelling, Minnesota. He applied and was accepted for the U.S. Army Air Force's aviation cadet program in December of 1941, and finally graduated from flight school at Luke Field, Arizona with the rating of pilot, on May 20, 1943. After extensive training in the United States in P-39's, P-40's, and finally P-38's, Purdy was sent to the Southwest Pacific with an assignment with the 433rd Fighter Squadron, 475th Fighter Group.

Seeing combat over New Guinea and the Philippines, Jack scored his first confirmed kill on May 16, 1944. While flying his P-38 nicknamed "Miss Wyandotte," Jack was able to spot and engage several Ki-43 "Oscar" fighters over Noemfoor Island, and in the melee shot one of them down in flames. Purdy did not score again until December 5, 1944, when he claimed two Japanese dive bombers over the Philippine Islands. On December 7, 1944, Purdy was directed to lead an escort mission for a PBY floatplane. The four P-38's, along with the massive PBY, scanned the blue waves of the South Pacific for hours looking for signs of downed aviators in the area. They found no pilots, but they did come across a Japanese

Naval convoy with between 25 and 30 "Oscar" fighters circling above. Though Purdy knew his men were outnumbered, he led them in and attacked the enemy formation. In his first pass Jack got hits on an Oscar, and seconds later shot down another. Seeing that none of the P-38's had sustained damage yet, he ordered his pilots to come in for another pass. Purdy soon spotted two Japanese fighters at low altitude, and surprised them with a violent burst of machine gun fire. A Japanese plane exploded and dove into sea, giving Jack his fifth kill and therefore making him an ace. The American planes, by now dangerously low on fuel, reformed and retuned to base. Purdy's P-38 ran out of fuel before he reached the 475th airfield,and he was forced to crash-land on a sandbar not far from an island called Cabugan Grande. Within minutes, several friendly natives paddled a canoe out to what was left of Jack's P-38, and offered him a ride back to their village. Purdy accepted, and was treated to a tribal feast before a PBY arrived to pick him up about 90 minutes later. Though still smarting from the bruises he had received during his encounter with the South Pacific sandbar, Purdy shot down two Mitsubishi "Zero" fighters over Mindanao Island on December 17, 1944. These victories proved to be his last, leaving his score at 7 confirmed and one damaged.

January 9, 1945 was perhaps the most eventful day of Purdy's life. While leading the 475th Fighter Group on a bombing mission, Jack's plane was hit by ground fire as he neared one of the target bridges near Luzon. After surviving a harrowing crash behind enemy lines, Purdy was rescued by friendly guerillas who treated his wounds and took excellent care of him for over 16 days until he was picked up by an American PBY "Catalina" Flying Boat. This mission, number 184 for Purdy, proved to be the last of his career, as he was soon sent back to the United States for recuperation.

After World War II, Purdy separated from the U.S. Armed Forces, but stayed active in the American Fighter Aces Association, eventually serving as President of the organization. He also founded and became CEO of the Dayton Showcase Company, and served on the board of nomination for the National Aviation Hall of Fame. A recipient of the Distinguished Flying Cross with 2 oak leaf clusters, the Purple Heart, and the Air Medal with 6 oak leaf clusters, Purdy died on September 8, 2003 at his home in Dayton, Ohio.

GERALD E. TYLER
7 victories
Hart

GERALD EDISON TYLER was born on October 18, 1921 in Hart, Michigan. As a youngster, Jerry's family moved to Kalamazoo where he would later attend Western Michigan University before volunteering his services to the U.S. Army Air Forces in April of 1942.

After graduating from flight school in April 1943, Tyler was assigned the position of P-39 flight instructor at Foster Field, Texas. Less than a year later, he was attached to the newly formed 357th Fighter Group which was about to ship out for England. When the 357th "Yoxford Boys" Fighter Group arrived in Europe in February, 1944, Tyler had only a few hours of flying time in the P-51 Mustang under his belt. Nevertheless; he began flying combat missions over enemy territory, and downed his first enemy aircraft, an ME-109, over Leipzing on June 29, 1944. His second and third kills came on July 5th and August 24th, respectively.

During the German invasion of Holland in September 1944, Tyler's achievements in aerial combat came to a peak. On the 18th of the month he shot down three ME-109 fighters and an FW-190 to become an ace. One day later he added another ME-109 to his record, which proved to be his final victory. By the time Germany surrendered in May, 1945, Tyler had racked up seven confirmed victories against German aircraft in the air. He had to his name a full list of decorations, including two

Distinguished Flying Crosses, twelve Air Medals, and the French Croix de Guerre.

Following World War II, Tyler's military service saw him graduate from the Squadron Officer's School, the Air Command and Staff College, and both Army and Air Force schools for special training as a fighter nuclear weapons specialist. After his retirement from the Air Force as a Lieutenant Colonel, Tyler held the positions of General Manager and Vice President of Cavalier Aircraft Corporation in Sarasota, Florida. Mr. Tyler passed away on July 21, 1988, having dedicated nearly all of his adult life to aviation.

EDWARD T. WATERS
7 Victories
Highland Park

THOUGH HE WAS BORN IN CAMBORNE, CORNWALL, ENGLAND, Edward Trebell Waters came to the United States in the mid 1920's at the age of five. His family settled in Highland Park, Michigan, where Waters would spend the rest of his childhood. Having just completed 1 ½ years of law school at Wayne University, Waters began his military career when he was drafted into the Army as a Private at Fort Custer. He later transferred to the Army Air Corps and was assigned to the aviation cadet training program, from which he graduated on September 29, 1942. Before shipping overseas, Waters was sent to Glendaale, California where he checked out in the P-38 *Lightning* and was assigned to the 82nd Fighter Group stationed in Algeria. He arrived at his base and flew his first combat mission on January 1, 1943.

Credited with damaging an ME-109 fighter on March 1, 1943, Waters scored his first kill when he shot down an Italian Cant Z. 1007 tri-motor bomber near Egadi Island. He added an Italian Breda 20 on April 17, and shot down a German ME-109 on May 20. In the month of June, Waters added three kills to his record, including another ME-109 on the 18th, an Italian MC.202 fighter on the 28th, and a German FW-109 on the 30th. His final victory came on July 10 when he shot down an ME-109 over Sicily. During his combat career, Waters earned the

Distinguished Flying Cross and the Air Medal with 14 Oak Leaf Clusters.

Returning to the States, Waters served as a pilot instructor and later as a test pilot before leaving the service as a Captain on December 15, 1945. In later years, Waters completed his education at the University of California and worked in a number of aeronautics-related positions, retiring as manager of Customer Relations for American Airlines. He now lives in Pryor, Oklahoma.

JOHN M. WESOLOWSKI
7 victories
Detroit

JOHN MAXWELL WESOLOWSKI was born on March 8, 1919 in Detroit. He attended Lawrence Institute of Technology and Wayne State University before enlisting in the Navy on December 30, 1940, and was subsequently assigned to training as a fighter pilot, which he completed on October 2, 1941. John's first military assignment took him aboard the USS *Wasp*, where he flew F4F *Wildcats* with VF-5. At the outbreak of World War II, Wesolowski was transferred to the USS *Saratoga*, where he served until the ship was torpedoed on September 11, 1942. John, along with the other pilots of VF-5 then received orders to act as a land-based unit, operating from Henderson Field on Guadalcanal. A key objective in the South Pacific, Henderson Field would prove to become one of the most contested pieces of real estate during World War II. Between August 1942 and February 1943, it was primarily defended by a group of American pilots like Wesolowski who would collectively become known as the "Cactus Air Force" for the prickly plant that served as Henderson's codename.

Just one day after arriving at the island on September 12, Wesolowski shot down a Japanese torpedo bomber over Guadalcanal. Two more enemy planes fell to the guns of his *Wildcat* the next day, and by the end of the week John's score of kills stood at five confirmed. Though he was now an ace, Wesolowski's hot streak was interrupted almost as quickly as it began due to a developing case of malaria which eventually brought about his evacuation from Guadalcanal. Sent back to the States to recuperate, Wesolowski found himself serving as a flight instructor when his orders came in January of 1945 that assigned him to VBF-9 on the USS *Yorktown*. Having checked out the F6F *Hellcat*, Wesolowski flew missions in support of the invasion of Okinawa, and downed a Japanese fighter on April 11 to score his first kill in almost 2 ½ years. On May 28, 1945 he concluded his combat record with the destruction of an "Oscar" fighter over the Pacific.

Following World War II, John stayed in the military, serving until his retirement at the rank of Commander in 1963. During his career he earned two awards of the Distinguished Flying Cross and received the Air Medal on nine different occasions. Wesolowski graduated from the University of Nebraska in 1964, and joined the Lockheed Corporation where he supervised ordinance subsystem development on submarine missiles, retiring in 1980.

MERL W. DAVENPORT
6.25 victories
Sterling Heights

MERL WILLIAM "BUTCH" DAVENPORT was born in Sterling, Michigan on March 14, 1918. Joining the Navy on January 7, 1941, he completed the Navy's flight training course in early 1942 and was assigned in 1943 to VF-17 flying F4U *Corsairs.* The squadron was later sent to the Solomon Islands, and operated from a base on New Georgia and later on Bougainville from October 27, 1943 to March 4, 1944.

Lt. Davenport got his first taste of aerial combat on November 6, 1943, when he chared credit with three other pilots for shooting down a Japanese "Betty" bomber 15 miles southwest of Bougainville. Two weeks later, he splashed two "Zeke" fighters at Empress Augusta Bay, and downed two more "Zekes" on January 30, 1944 over Simpson Harbor. Six days later he downed his fifth Zeke off Cape Gazelle to become an ace. His sixth and last kill came on February 10, over Vanakanan Island before he was shipped back to the United States in March.

Remaining in the service after the war, Davenport served as a test pilot, setting a "time-to-climb" record in the F8F *Bearcat* by reaching an altitude of 10,000 feet in only 96 seconds. A recipient of the two Distinguished Flying Crosses, Merl Davenport died of cancer in Dexter, Michigan on September 19, 1989.

ARTHUR R. CONANT
6 victories
Crystal Falls

ARTHUR R. (ROG) CONANT was born on October 21, 1918 in Crystal Falls, Michigan. He graduated from the University of Wisconsin in 1941, before joining the US Marine Corps flight training program, and won his aviator's wings in Corpus Christi, Texas on June 25, 1942. Assigned to VMF-215, flying F4U Corsairs in the Solomon Islands, Conant scored his first victories on August 25, 1943 with the confirmed destruction of two Japanese fighters and two more probably destroyed. On September 1he scored again, this time downing a "Zeke" fighter just three miles west of Vella Lavella Island. A brief R&R period followed, after which came a string of strafing and air-to-ground missions for VMF-215. Aerial combat picked up again in January of 1944, with Conant downing three more "Zekes" before the end of the month to conclude his scoring.

Decorated with five Distinguished Flying Crosses, 10 Air Medals, and the Navy Commendation Medal, Captain Conant returned to the United States and was discharged from the Marines in 1945. However, his military service would not end there, as he was subsequently recalled to active duty in 1950 for service in the Korean War. Conant spent one year flying the F9F *Panther* on ground attack missions in Korea, returning to the States in 1952 to work as a test pilot. During an air-to-air missile test for the Douglas Aircraft Corporation, Conant shot down five

65

unmanned drones in one day, and later joked that he was probably the only US ace to have shot down five American planes as well.

Conant continued work as an active test pilot and consultant for McDonnell Douglas right up to his retirement from the industry in 1985. Today, he lives with his wife Evelyn in Seattle, Washington.

URBAN L. DREW
6 victories
Detroit

BORN IN DETROIT, MICHIGAN on March 21, 1944, Urban Leonard "Ben" Drew enlisted in the USAAF in October of 1942, and graduated from flight school with class 43-I at Meriana, Florida. Lieutenant Drew was then assigned to the position of P-51 flight instructor, and held this position until May of 1944 when he was assigned to the 361st Fighter Group then stationed in England. By the time he arrived in Europe, Drew had already accumulated an incredible 700 hours of flight time in the P-51. This experience paid off, considering that most other pilots had an average of 60 flight hours when they were sent into combat. Drew's flying expertise brought him an ME-109 kill on August 25, 1944 to open his account. Following up with another ME-109 kill on September 11, Drew ran his score to three with the destruction of an HE-111 bomber on the 18th. It was on this same mission that Drew spotted "the biggest airplane in the world" moored on Lake Schaal: a BV-238 V-1 six-engined flying boat. With two wingmen at his side, Drew dove his P-51 into an attack and flew his way into history by sinking the massive craft.

During his tour of duty with the 361st, Drew logged a total of 75 combat missions and was credited with a total of 6 German aircraft shot down. His final successes came when he shot down two ME-262 jets on October 7, 1944 over a German held airfield in Europe. This feat made Drew the first American airman to destroy two enemy jets in one day, and would eventually earn him an Air Force Cross. Unfortunately, this award was not officially bestowed until 1983 due to errors in the records keeping process.

At the completion of his combat tour in Europe, Drew was transferred to the 414th Fighter Group based on Iwo Jima in the Pacific. With this unit, Drew participated in missions against the Japanese while flying the P-47, but never clamed another kill.

After the War, Drew was instrumental in the founding of the Michigan Air National Guard, serving as Vice Wing Commander of the 127th Fighter Wing. He later became the first Air Adjutant General for the State of Michigan, before retiring from military service. Drew would later go on to establish a successful aviation business in South Africa. A holder of the Air Force Cross, 2 Distinguished Flying Crosses, and 14 Air Medals, Ben Drew now lives in retirement in California.

CHARLES E. EDINGER
6 victories
Onaway

AN ACE WHOSE STORY IS UNIQUE among those of aviators from Michigan, Charles Emmanuel Edinger was born on April 17, 1916 in Onaway,, Michigan. He enlisted in the Canadian Air Force on May 12, 1941, more than six months before America was attacked at Pearl Harbor. One of very few American aviators who served exclusively in a foreign Air Force during World War II, he was assigned the rank of pilot officer after graduating from flight training in February of 1942. After serving as a flight instructor in England for over two and a half years, Edinger was finally attached to the RAF's 410 Squadron, and began flying combat missions over Europe in the twin engine deHavilid *Mosquito*.

Teamed with radar operator Charles Vassen, Edinger claimed his first aerial victory on June 18, 1944 by downing a German Ju-188 bomber over the English Channel. He shot down another '188 on July 4, but did not score again until September 17, when he and Vassen intercepted an unidentified aircraft and forced it to crash without firing a shot during the ensuing chase.

The team continued their string of success on October 6, downing a Ju-88 bomber of Holland. Edinger became an ace on December 18, 1944, when he shot down another German bomber just south of Bonninghardt, Germany, and completed his scoring on

Christmas Eve with the destruction of a Ju-87 Stuka dive bomber near Wassenburg.

Edinger left 410 Squadron on April 7, 1945, and returned to Canada on September 15. He was released from the military on October 26, 1945, having been decorated with the British Distinguished Flying Cross. Though little is known of Edinger's life after the war, it is certain that his service during World War II played a decisive role in the air war over Europe.

LELAND A. LARSON
6 victories
Whitemore

LELAND ALSON LARSON was born on April 10, 1923 in Whitemore, Michigan. He enlisted in the US Army Air Force and later was awarded the wings of an aviator on February 1, 1944. Having trained in P-51's converted into F-6 reconnaissance aircraft, Larson was assigned to the 10th Photographic Group and began flying photo missions that penetrated deep into heart of German – occupied territory.

On January 14, 1945, Larson downed an FW-190 in a chance dogfight over Koblenz, Germany. After a dry spell of three months, action picked up in March with Larson shooting down two ME-109's and an FW-190 before the month was out. On April 8, he became an ace with the destruction of a Ju-87 dive bomber and an HE-111medium bomber north of Dresden.

Two days after Germany surrendered on May 6, 1945, Larson and one other F-6 pilot made contact with two FW-190 aircraft apparently en route to Switzerland. Pulling along side the '190's, the Americans waggled their wings in an attempt to lead them to an airfield. Not about to surrender, the Germans began to take evasive action and eventually crashed their aircraft into the forest below in a desperate attempt to escape the Americans. Though no shots were fired during the engagement, this episode proved to be the final encounter between American and German aircraft in World War II.

By the time Lt. Larson was shipped back to the United States, the had flown a total of 77 combat missions over enemy territory, and had been awarded the Distinguished Flying Cross, and the Air Medal with 19 Oak Leaf Clusters. He later separated from the military, and returned to his home state of Michigan, passing away on September 30, 1990.

JAMES D. MUGAVERO
6 victories
Port Huron

A NATIVE OF PORT HURON, James Dennis Mugavero was born on July 3, 1920. He attended Port Huron Junior College before enlisting in the US Army following the United States' entry into World War II. He later applied for pilot training, was accepted, and was then sent to Arcadia Field, Florida for Primary Flight Training. He attended Basic Flight School at Bainbridge Field, Georgia, and won his commission as a second Lieutenant on October 1, 1943 in Marianna, Florida.

Following an additional period of training in the P-47, Mugavero was sent to the Southwest Pacific Theater to serve with the 35th Fighter Group, arriving with the unit in January of 1944. His first victories come on October 14, 1944 while flying escort for a bomber strike over the Japanese held island of Borneo. Engaging a formation of four Ki-43 "Oscar" fighters on this mission, Mugavero fired off a short burst at the lead plane and saw it explode in a huge ball of flame. Peeling off into a dive he spotted another "Oscar" and opened fire on it as soon as it came into range. As black smoke began to pour from the engine of the crippled Japanese plane, Mugavero watched the aircraft disintegrate as it dove into the ground.

In subsequent aerial battles, Mugavero was credited with downing two enemy fighters in November of 1944, and claimed his final kills on January 13, 1945 by flaming two more Japanese planes on a single mission. After retuning to the United States, Mugavero parted ways with the military, but was later recalled by the government to serve in the Korean conflict. He then remained in the Air Force until his retirement at the rank of Lieutenant Colonel in May of 1970. During his military career, Mugavero was decorated with the Silver Star, the Distinguished Flying Cross, and three Air Medals.

ZENNETH A. POND
6 victories
Hillsdale County

BORN ON DECEMBER 7, 1919 in Hillsdale County, Michigan, Zenneth Arthur Pond attended Jackson Junior College where he received his private pilot's license before entering the United States Marine Corps. He graduated from flight school and was commissioned as a second lieutenant in Corpus Christi, Texas on April 6, 1942 before shipping out with Marine Fighter Squadron 223 for the island of Guadalcanal in the South Pacific.

Under the command of legendary fighter ace Major John L. Smith, Pond flew his first combat missions in August of 1942, piloting an F4F *Wildcat* from the coral runway on Guadalcanal called Henderson Field. He shot down his first Japanese aircraft on August 24, downing two single-engine dive bombers and a *Zero* fighter over the island. He scored again on the 29th, this time claiming an unidentified Japanese fighter, and made ace the following day with the destruction of another *Zero* in the Guadalcanal area. Pond claimed what would be his last aerial kill on September 5, shooting down a twin-engine "Betty" bomber over Henderson Field. Just five days later, Pond failed to return from a combat sortie and was later declared missing in action.

For his heroic achievement in just eighteen days of combat on Guadalcanal, Pond was posthumously awarded the Marine Corps' second highest medal for valor: the

Navy Cross. No trace was ever found of Pond or his plane, and the events leading to the death of this American hero remain a mystery to this day.

HERMAN W. VISSCHER
6 victories
Portage

A NATIVE OF PORTAGE, MICHIGAN, Herman William Visscher was born on December 27, 1920. He enlisted in the U.S. Army Air Corps at Selfridge Field, Michigan on November 1, 1939 as a private. Visscher won his Air Force wings of silver on March 7, 1942. One of very few enlisted fighter pilots, his rank at that time was Staff Sergeant. Visscher eventually earned a commission in the Army Air Force as a Second Lieutenant on September 20, 1942, and soon afterwards began flying combat missions with the 82nd Fighter Group in North Africa. In his P-38 fighter, Herman shot down his first enemy aircraft, a JU-52 transport plane on January 17, 1943. Another kill followed on February 3rd, this time in the form of an ME-109 fighter. He shot down another ME-109 on February 28, and scored his fourth kill on May 13th. On the 19th of May, 1943, Visscher rounded out his World War II scoring with the destruction of another ME-109. By the time he returned to the United States in August, 1945, he had flown 80 combat missions and had logged 340 hours of combat flying time.

During the Korean War, Visscher was again called upon to serve his country. He completed 106 combat missions in F-86 fighter jets with the 51st Fighter Interceptor Wing, and was credited with the destruction of one MiG-15 on September 15, 1952.

Visscher retired from military service in Battle Creek, Michigan on June 1, 1966 with the rank of Major. During his 27 years as a member of the U.S. Armed forces, he received the Distinguished Flying Cross with three Oak leaf clusters, the Air Medal with seventeen oak leak clusters, and the Army Commendation Medal. He now lives in Mattawan, Michigan.

ROBERT E. WELCH
6 Victories
Brown City

A NATIVE OF BROWN CITY, MICHIGAN, Robert Eadon Welch was born on August 4, 1923. He enlisted in the Army Air Forces on March 10, 1943 and was accepted for aviation cadet training soon afterwards. He received his aviator's wings and a commission as a second lieutenant at Aloe Field, Texas on January 7, 1944. Following fighter transition, he was assigned to the 343rd Fighter Squadron of the 55th Fighter Group, operating out of Nuthampstead, England.

Welch scored his first victory on September 13, 1944, shooting down an ME-109 and damaging a second. Flying his P-51 coded CY-O and bearing the phrase "Wings of the Mornin'" across the cowl, he shot another '109 on November 24, and downed his third enemy aircraft exactly one month later on Christmas Eve. The morning of December 25, 1944 saw Welch participate in a combat mission over Koblenz, Germany on which he destroyed two more enemy aircraft to join the elite ranks of fighter aces. By April 1945, Welch had been promoted to the rank of Captain, and had nearly completed his tour of duty in Europe. On April 17, he flew his final combat mission and shot down his last plane, an FW-190 over Dresden, to complete his illustrious combat record that also featured the Silver Star, the Distinguished Flying Cross, an the Air Medal with 25 Oak Leaf Clusters.

After World War II, Welch separated from the military, but later joined the 172nd Fighter Squadron of the Michigan Air National Guard in Battle Creek, Michigan. It was with the National Guard that Welch logged many additional hours in the P-51, eventually being recalled to active duty for service in Korea. While participating in pre-combat training on March 23, 1951 at Luke Air Force Base, Arizona, Major Welch was killed in a mid-air collision while leading a flight of four aircraft.

MURRAY WINFIELD
6 victories
Detroit

MURRAY WINFIELD was born in Detroit on May 1, 1924, and joined the Navy on July 16, 1942. Assigned to flight school, he received his designation as a fighter pilot on November 1, 1943, and was subsequently attached to VF-17, flying F6F *Hellcats* off of the USS *Hornet* (CV-12) in the Pacific.

Lt. (J.G.) Winfield was credited with his first aerial victory on March 19, 1945 on a fighter sweep over southern Japan when he shared credit for a destroyed "Oscar" fighter and another damaged. Two days later, his flight division jumped a formation of Japanese "Betty" bombers near Kyushu, Japan. In the melee that followed, Winfield was credited with the destruction of 4.5 of the enemy planes, therefore gaining the coveted status of ace. He claimed his final kill, a "Frank" fighter over the Ryukyu Islands on April 16, 1945 to conclude his scoring. Awarded the Silver Star, 3 Distinguished Flying Crosses, and 4 Air Medals, Winfield elected to stay in the military after and retired from the Navy in July of 1965 at the rank of Lieutenant Commander.

WALTER J. KORALESKI
5.53 Victories
Detroit

BORN IN DETROIT ON APRIL 30, 1920, Walter Joseph Koraleski was a third-year aeronautical engineering student at the University of Detroit when he entered the Army Air Forces on November 3, 1941. After graduating from Class 42-E on May 20, 1942 in Victoria, Texas, he was assigned to the 50th Fighter Group at Key Field, Mississippi for fighter training in the P-47 *Thunderbolt*. Later transferred to the 355th Fighter Group, Koraleski participated in the group's first combat mission on September 14, 1943. Though he flew missions on a regular basis, Koraleski did not claim his first kill until March 6, 1944, when he shot down two ME-109's and shared credit for a third over Berlin. He claimed another '109 ten days later while breaking up a German attack on a formation of B-17 bombers over Augsburg, and ran his score to 4.5 with an FW-190 kill in early October.

On April 5, 1944, the 355th Fighter Group broke all records set up to that time for kills in the European Theater by annihilating 51 enemy aircraft on one mission. Koraleski shared credit for three of the planes shot down that day, bringing his final score to 5.53 aerial victories to become the 355th's second fighter ace. On April 15, 1944, the 355th Fighter Group flew an escort mission over two enemy-held airfields in Germany. It was on the return trip that Koraleski's P-51 "Miss Thunder" lost oil pressure, forcing the American ace to bail out of his stricken craft.

Captured by the Nazi ground forces, Koraleski was destined to spend the rest of the war as a prisoner in Stalag Luft III.

After his liberation at the war's end, Koraleski remained in the Air Force and later flew combat missions during the Korean War as a member of the 18th Fighter-Bomber Wing. He retired in November 1968, having attained the rank of Lieutenant Colonel. During his military career, Koraleski was decorated with the Silver Star, the Distinguished Flying Cross with 2 Oak Leaf Clusters, and the Air Medal with 3 Oak Leaf Clusters.

WILLIAM L. HOOD, JR.
5.5 Victories
Kalamazoo

WILLIAM LESLIE HOOD, JR. was born on May 7, 1924 in Kalamazoo, Michigan. After completing the Navy's pilot training course on July 16, 1943, he was commissioned a Second Lieutenant in the United States Marine Corps, and was assigned to VMF-323. Arriving in the Pacific in October of 1944, Hood began flying combat missions from Espiritu Santo Island in the F4U *Corsair*. VMF-323 moved to Manus Island in March, 1945, and later based at Kadena Field on Okinawa, where Hood would participate in some of the most intense aerial combat seen during World War II.

On April 22, 1945, Hood's flight division of four *Corsairs* encountered a large enemy attack force 50 miles north of Aguni Shima. Intercepting the attackers, Hood tore into the Japanese formation and downed two fighters in the first seconds of the engagement. He shared credit for three more Val dive bombers that day, and damaged two more, opening his aerial combat record in a big way. Six days later, he was involved in another dogfight in the Okinawa area, and this time downed tow Val dive bombers to become an ace. These kills proved to be Hood's last, as he was shipped back to the United States for leave soon afterwards. Decorated with two Distinguished Flying Crosses and two Air Medals, Hood was killed in the crash of a private plane near Benton Harbor, Michigan on August 4, 1946.

JOHN B. MASS, JR.
5.5 Victories
Lansing

BORN ON MAY 19, 1920 IN LANSING, MICHIGAN, John Bernard Maas, Jr. grew up in Grosse Point. He attended Notre Dame for three years and became a Naval aviation cadet in June of 1941. Upon his graduation from flight school, he was commissioned a second lieutenant in the Marine Corps and was assigned to VMF-112. Shipped to Guadalcanal in November of 1942, he arrived at Henderson Field and began flying combat missions in the F4F *Wildcat*.

On November 12, 1942, Mass and several other pilots from VMF-112 encountered a formation of "Betty" torpedo bombers coming in over Guadalcanal. In the ensuing action, Mass was credited with the destruction of one enemy plane, chalking up his first confirmed victory. Two days later, he downed a *Zero* fighter over the Russell Islands to bring his score to two. After enduring a long dry spell, Maas finally scored again on January 31, 1943 with a *Zero* kill over Vella Gulf. Now flying a F4U Corsair, Maas was again credited with the destruction of a *Zero* on May 31, and followed up with a probable kill the next day.

Having been promoted to Major after a stateside rest tour, Mass was reassigned to another *Corsair* unit, VMF-322, and retuned to combat in April of 1945. On May 25, while chasing a flock of "Tojo" fighters in the Okinawa

Area, Maas was credited with downing one enemy aircraft, and shared credit for destroying another.

Returning to the States in October of 1945, Maas served as assistant Naval attaché in Venezuela from 1946-1948, and again saw combat during the Korean War. In 1958, Maas assumed command of VMA-332, flying A4D Skyhawks. He subsequently served in a number of command and staff assignments before retiring as a Colonel in June of 1968. During his exciting career, Mass was decorated with three Distinguished Flying Crosses, the Bronze Star with "V" device, and nine Air Medals. Recently, Maas served as director of the Marine Corps Aviation Association for over 10 years, and now resides in Fredericksburg, Virginia with his wife Natalie.

MICHAEL G. H. MCPHARLIN
5.5 Victories
Hastings

MICHAEL G. H. MCPHARLIN was born in 1916 in Hastings, Michigan. In 1940, while studying medicine in Illinois, he volunteered his services to Britain's Royal Air Force as a pilot. He was accepted and trained to fly *Spitfire* aircraft before being assigned to the 71 RAF squadron. This unit was composed almost entirely of Americans who volunteered to fly and fight for England. Formed in September of 1940, No. 71 Squadron, along with the 121 and 133 RAF Units, would become collectively known as the "Eagle Squadrons."

While serving with the RAF, Michael McPharlin gained combat experience over Europe before the United States officially joined the war. He was credited with the destruction of 1.5 German aircraft on August 19, 1942, which proved to be his first and only kills achieved while flying for England. When the Eagle squadrons were disbanded in September of 1942, McPharlin was transferred to the US Army Air Force's 339th Fighter Group and with this unit resumed aerial operations against the Luftwaffe, now flying a P-51 *Mustang*. He eventually added four more kills to his record, becoming a full-fledged fighter ace on May 28, 1944.

As the Allies began their invasion of Normandy on June 6, 1944, McPharlin, by now a Major, was participating in a combat sortie over the Dreux, France area. At one point in the mission, he radioed to his squadron mates and said that he was aborting because his left magneto was out and the engine was running rough. It was the last time anyone saw or heard from him, as he was reported missing in action later that day.

During his brief but heroic career, Michael G. H. McPharlin was decorated with the Distinguished Flying Cross and three Air Medals. His record of service stands to this day as a fine example of airmanship.

DONOVAN F. SMITH
5.5 Victories
Dowagiac

DONOVAN FRANCIS SMITH was born in Dowagiac, Michigan on October 2, 1922, and graduated from Niles High School, in 1940. He entered the aviation cadet program in January of 1942 and upon completion of pilot training on October 8, 1942 was commissioned a second lieutenant in the U.S. Army Air Corps.

In November 1942, he joined the 61st Fighter Squadron, 56th Fighter Group, in England, subsequently becoming the squadron commander. Smith remained with the 61st Fighter Squadron throughout his combat duty in the European Theater of Operations, which lasted from March 1943 to February 1945. During this time he flew 123 combat missions for a total of 385 flying hours in the P-47 Thunderbolt aircraft. Smith downed his first enemy aircraft on December 11, 1943, when he flamed two ME-110 fighters and an FW-190 on a bomber escort over Emden. He later shot down a pair of ME-110's on February 20, 1944, and shared credit for an FW-109 two days later to complete his scoring.

Smith returned to the United States in March 1945 and was assigned as project officer, Tactics Division, Army Air Forces Board, at Orlando Army Air Field, Fla. In November 1945 he was transferred to Headquarters Army Air Forces, Washington, D.C., as air staff officer, Intelligence. He later served as a U.S. Air Force/Royal

Air Force exchange officer, from August 1949 to September 1950 and served as commander, Number 1 Fighter Squadron, Royal Air Force, at Tangmere, England.

In October 1966, Smith was named chief, Air Force Advisory Group, Military Assistance Command in Vietnam. He served the next 18 months as chief adviser to the Republic of Vietnam Air Force. In May 1968 he returned to the United States and became vice commander, Ninth Air Force, Shaw Air Force Base, S.C. He assumed duties as commander of the Nineteenth, "Suitcase," Air Force at Seymour Johnson Air Force Base, N.C., in August 1969.

Promoted to Lieutenant General on July 1, 1973, Smith retired from the military in 1974, and died on September 10th of that year. His final resting place is on the grounds of the US Air Force Academy in Colorado Springs, Colorado.

During his distinguished career in his nation's service, Donovan Smith was decorated with the Distinguished Service Cross, Distinguished Service Medal, Legion of Merit, Distinguished Flying Cross with three oak leaf clusters, Air Medal with eight oak leaf clusters, and the Air Force Commendation Medal.

WALTER A. WOOD
5.5 Victories
Ionia

BORN ON JULY 4, 1921, IN IONIA, MICHIGAN, Walter A. Wood enlisted in the US Navy on May 28, 1942. Graduating from flight school on August 7, 1943, he was assigned to VF-20 and embarked for the Pacific on board the USS Enterprise. Flying the F6F *Hellcat*, Wood scored his first aerial victory on October 12, 1944, when he destroyed a Japanese "Tojo" fighter over the Island of Formosa. He scored again three days later on a combat air patrol mission over the Philippines, downing 3 enemy aircraft and sharing credit for a fourth when his squadron was vectored to intercept the large enemy formation.

While participating in a photo-reconnaissance flight over Manila on October 18, Wood's division of four aircraft was met by heavy aerial opposition. Hopelessly outnumbered, the Americans fought savagely for their lives. Though Wood was able to destroy an "Oscar" fighter to make ace that day, he himself was shot down and killed by a Japanese airman during the melee.

Though his career was cut short by his untimely death at the age of 23, Walter Wood managed to become one of the most decorated aces from Michigan, earning the Navy Cross, the Silver Star, the Distinguished Flying Cross, Three Air Medals, a Purple Heart, and the Presidential Unit Citation.

MELVIN M. PRITCHARD
5.25 Victories
Gaylord

MELVIN MERL PRITCHARD was born on April 18, 1919 in Gaylord, Michigan. He received a private pilot's license at Northern Michigan University in 1940 and entered Navy flight training in early 1942. After graduating on October 16, 1942, Pritchard was assigned to the USS *Enterprise*, where he would fly F6F *Hellcats* with VF-20.

Promoted to lieutenant (j.g.) on January 1, 1944, Pritchard scored his first victories on October 15, 1944 when his division was vectored to intercept an incoming enemy formation. Diving into the fight, Pritchard quickly splashed two *Zeke* fighters and minutes later shared credit for a fourth. He again scored on October 28, sharing credit for a "Tojo" fighter over Ormoc, and later downed two "Oscars" over Clark Field in the Philippines on November 13. Completing his record the next day with a shared "Myrt" floatplane, Pritchard was sent back to the United States to end his combat tour.

After the war, Pritchard served as a test pilot and contract negotiations officer for the Bureau of Aeronautics. He later commanded VF-11 onboard the USS *Franklin D. Roosevelt* (CVA-42), and was promoted to his final rank of Commander in 1956. Pritchard retired from the Navy on June 30, 1969 and passed away on September 10, 1994 in Los Angeles, California. His decorations and awards included the Silver Star, 2 Distinguished Flying Crosses, and 8 Air Medals.

FRANK B. BALDWIN
5 victories
Flint

FRANK BERNARD BALDWIN, a native of Flint, Michigan was born on February 20, 1920. As a young man, Baldwin attended Waynesboro Teacher's College in Pittsburg, Pennsylvania before joining the Marine Corps late in 1941. He was commissioned a Second Lieutenant on May 22, 1942 at Chorus Christi, Texas, and was soon assigned to VMF-221 as an F4F "Wildcat" pilot. In the Spring of 1943, Baldwin's unit arrived on the island of Guadalcanal, where he and his squadron mates would spend the next few months flying combat missions out of the crudely constructed Henderson Airfield; a key objective in the Pacific Theatre.

Before returning home to the U.S. for a rest tour, Baldwin made a name for himself as fighter pilot in aerial brawls over Guadalcanal, Bougainville, Savo Island, and Tarawa. This experience would pay off in 1944 when he was assigned the position of flight leader with his old unit VMF-221, now stationed on the aircraft carrier USS Bunker Hill. Throughout his second tour of duty in the Pacific, Baldwin led dozens of combat missions over enemy territory while equipped with the new F4U Corsair. He witnessed the horror of kamikaze attacks on American shipping and participated in many dangerous raids over the Homeland Islands of Japan. Baldwin eventually rose to command Fighting Squadron 221, having been promoted to the rank of Major late in the war. Upon his final return to the United States in 1945, Baldwin's tally for aircraft destroyed stood at 5 destroyed, 1 probably destroyed, and 1 ¼ damaged. Among his many awards and decorations were two Distinguished Flying Crosses, seven Air Medals, and a Presidential Unit Citation.

Following his service in the Marine Corps, Baldwin was employed for many years with the B.F. Goodrich Corporation. He and his wife "Rebel" raised four children in their marriage of some 58 years. Frank Baldwin passed away in Akron, Ohio on April 17, 2004.

RAYMOND M. BANK
5 victories
Kendall

BORN ON A FARM NEAR KENDALL, MICHIGAN ON MARCH 15, 1924, Raymond Matt Bank moved to Chicago with his family when he was a young boy. Raymond enlisted in the United States Army Air Force in September, 1942, and graduated from flight school with a commission as a Second Lieutenant in August 1943. He served as a Basic Flight Instructor, and later moved on to the position of gunnery instructor, and finally was a fighter transition instructor in P-40's. Bank soon received a combat assignment with the 357th Fighter Group, and shipped out to England in August, 1944. His orders put him in the 364th Fighter Squadron, 357th Fighter Group, which was then a unit in the 8th Air Force. Bank began flying missions in his P-51D Mustang that he had nicknamed "Fireball," but did not shoot his first German airplane down until Christmas Eve, 1944. Bank shot down his next German planes on January 14, 1945. In this fight which took place south of Schwerin, Germany, Bank was able to claim three FW-190 fighters shot down, bringing his tally to four fighters destroyed.

March 2, 1945 saw Raymond Bank strafing German ground positions in the heart of Germany. When a formation of German fighters jumped the American pilots an air-to-air engagement resulted. After the smoke cleared, Bank had one more ME-109 to his credit. He was an Ace, but would not have long to enjoy it, for he was shot down moments later when his Mustang was hit by ground fire. Seeing that his P-51's hydraulic, coolant, and oil lines were no longer functional, Bank crash landed his stricken bird behind enemy lines. It was not long before he was taken prisoner and sent to Stalag Luft 7, and later Stalag Luft 3A prison camps. For over three months Ray lived as a POW until he was liberated by tanks of Patton's Third Army. He was then returned to the United States, and was again appointed flight instructor.

Bank left the active duty Air Force in 1947, but continued to serve in the Air Force Reserves. He attended the University of Illinois for two years before he was recalled to active duty in March of 1951, again as a flight instructor. Transitioning to multi-engine aircraft, Bank was trained as a B-47 pilot in 1954, and then spent over eleven years in the Strategic Air Command. He again saw combat in the Vietnam War, this time as a C-130 pilot. As a member of the 315th Tactical Airlift Squadron, he spent over three years in South East Asia. During this time he flew over 1,000 missions in and out of Vietnam. Raymond M. Bank retired from the U.S. Air Force in November of 1970 as a Major with 2 Distinguished Flying Crosses, 2 Purple Hearts and 11 Air Medals to his credit, along with over 10,000 hours of flight time. Bank, who is an active member of the American Fighter Aces Association, now lives with his wife Annette, in Gahanna, Ohio.

ROBERT M. BARKEY

5 Victories

Wyandotte

ROBERT MERRILL BARKEY was born on September 5, 1917 in Wyandotte, Michigan. He attended Michigan State University and later served as a member of the Wyandotte police department before offering his services to the Army Air Corps just after the Japanese attack on Pearl Harbor. Barkey graduated from flight school at Brooks Field, Texas on October 9, 1942, and was later sent to Key Field, Mississippi, where he trained in dive bombing and observation aircraft.

Late in 1943, Lt. Barkey was assigned to the 319th Fighter Squadron of the 325th Fighter Group. Known as the "Checkertail Clan," the 325th operated as a unit from the deserts of North Africa, flying P-40 *Warhawk* fighters against German and Italian targets in the Mediterranean area. After transitioning into P-47 aircraft in the latter part of 1943, the group was eventually moved to Italy where it joined the 15th Air Force.

The Checkertails began combat operations with the P-47 in mid-December of 1943. Flying his P-47 "Thunderbolt Lad," Barkey gained his first aerial victory on January 22, 1944 while flying top cover for the invasion of Anzio. On March 11, he downed an ME-109 over Padua, and followed up on the 18th with another ME-109 kill over Southern Italy. May 24, 1944 saw Barkey add another ME-109 to his record, this time downing the enemy aircraft while providing escort cover for a crippled B-17 bomber. He would go on to make ace just a few days later with the destruction of yet another ME-109 before being sent beck to the United States just ten days later to participate in a war bond drive.

Although released from active duty in November, 1945, Barkey remained in the Air Force Reserves, serving with the 242nd Tactical Control Wing. In 1951, Barkey was recalled to active duty, and served as commander of a squadron of F-84 *Thunderjets* at Bergstrom AFB, Texas. Retiring as a Major on December 11, 1959, Barkey continued to fly as a commercial pilot, and now lives in Monrovia, California with his wife Madelyn. Barkey is a holder of the Distinguished Flying Cross and the Air Medal with 12 Oak Leaf Clusters.

WILLIAM A. CARLTON
5 Victories
Saginaw

BORN IN SAGINAW, MICHIGAN ON JULY 30, 1915, William Ayles Carlton received his commission as a Marine Corps Second Lieutenant on July 16, 1941. Joining VMF-212, Carlton was subsequently stationed on the island of Barakoma in the fall of 1943, serving under the command of Major Stewart O'Niell. Though his squadron claimed a total of 58 aerial victories while supporting the Bougainville campaign, Carlton was only credited with one "Zeke" probably destroyed during this period.

Following the squadron's move to Torokina, Carlton enjoyed more success, downing a Japanese fighter in January of 1944 south of Rabaul. His best day in combat came on February 13, when he became engaged in an intense aerial battle over Rabaul. Carlton quickly flamed one of the lead *Zeros* on this mission and damaged a second before probably destroying a third enemy fighter. Less than three minutes later, he was credited with his second confirmed kill of the day, downing another *Zero*. As he climbed to regain lost altitude, Carlton was jumped by several more enemy fighters and shot one of them down for his third kill that day. He made ace just two days later by destroying a "Val" dive bomber over Bougainville.

Promoted to the rank of Major, Carlton was rotated back to the United States, later assuming command of

VMF-914 on August 14, 1944. He remained with this unit until the end of the war, and eventually left the service after a very successful career in uniform. Decorated with the Distinguished Flying Cross and two Air Medals, Carlton died on in June of 1995.

RICHARD E. DUFFY
5 victories
Walled Lake

RICHARD E. DUFFY was born on January 20, 1918 in Walled Lake, Michigan. After enlisting in the Army Air Corps, he graduated from flight school and was designated as the pilot of a P-40 aircraft. Assigned to the 314th Fighter Squadron, 324th Fighter Group, Duffy later shipped out with his unit for their destination of Tunisia.

After arriving in Africa, Duffy began flying combat missions in support of Allied operations in North Africa and Sicily. On the afternoon of April 18, 1943, Duffy formed up with 48 other P-40's over the Gulf of Tunis. Their mission was to intercept a large formation of 85+ German Ju-52 transport planes evacuating troops from combat. It was late evening before the Americans spotted their targets, splitting into two pairs as they dove into the fight. During the course of the next few minutes, American pilots racked up claims for over seventy-five German planes destroyed and many more damaged. This mission, which would become known as the "Palm Sunday Massacre," also had the distinction of producing history's first three Army Air Force "aces in one day." Among those three was Lt. Richard E. Duffy, who was credited with five Ju-52's destroyed and one damaged. Describing his attack on the enemy formations Duffy later said;

"They were so tightly packed that I had three in my sights at one time. I even got two with one machine gun burst. Those two collided and fell into the sea. The next one also crashed into the water with its engines smoking, and the other two were both flamers."

Duffy, who never claimed another kill during his career, was decorated with the Silver Star for his contributions to the success of the April 18th mission. By the war's end, he had also racked up seven awards of the Air Medal plus numerous campaign and service medals. As the first of three Michigan natives to become an ace in just one combat mission, Richard E. Duffy certainly earned himself a place in the illustrious history of the fighter ace.

JOHN W. FAIR
5 victories
Battle Creek

JOHN W. FAIR was born on November 19, 1920, and enlisted in the US Navy on April 16, 1941. He graduated from flight training and pinned on his gold aviator's wings in June of 1942, subsequently spending over a year as a flight training instructor inside the United States. By now an experienced pilot of an F6F *Hellcat* fighter plane, Fair was assigned to Navy Flying Squadron 80, and finally embarked for the Pacific aboard the aircraft carrier *USS Ticonderoga* in October of 1944. While participating in his very first combat mission on November 5, Fair's squadron encountered a number of Japanese aircraft in flight over the Philippines. During the ensuing fight, Fair accounted for the destruction of one Japanese fighter plane, and damaged a second. Less than a week later, he destroyed another enemy plane to bring his score of confirmed "kills" to two. Though he continued to fly missions on a regular basis, Fair did not score again until the morning of February 16, 1945, when he destroyed an impressive three Japanese aircraft during a dramatic aerial duel over Tokyo, Japan that lasted only a few minutes. With these kills, which proved to be the last of his career, Fair flew his way into the history books as one of America's prestigious Fighter Aces.

After the war, Fair elected to remain in the Navy, and also served with distinction during the Korean and Vietnam conflicts. He retired from the military on January

31, 1972, having attained the rank of Captain. During his military career which spanned over thirty years, Captain Fair received for his heroism the Silver Star Medal, the Legion of Merit with one Gold Star, the Distinguished Flying Cross, and the Air Medal with two Gold Stars. One of Battle Creek's most distinguished natives, Fair passed away in Orange Park, Florida on May 10, 1992, ending an exciting life which was dedicated to the defense and service of the United States of America.

ROBERT D. GIBB
5 victories
Detroit

BORN ON FEBRUARY 16, 1922 IN DETROIT, Robert Duncan Gibb joined the Army Air Forces as an aviation cadet on January 21, 1942. He graduated from flight school on October 9, 1942. Following fighter instruction the P-47, he was assigned to the 348th Fighter Group, which was stationed in the South Pacific under the command of legendary fighter ace Neel Kearby.

The 348th Fighter Group was awarded a rare Presidential Citation for its outstanding performance while covering the landings of Allied ground forces from December 16-31, 1943; dates that happened to coincide with Lt. Gibb's victories. While flying his P-47 out of an airfield on New Guinea, he scored his first kill on December 16, downing a "Zeke" fighter over Arawe. Just five days later, Gibb made ace with four "Val" dive bombers destroyed to conclude his brief combat record. During this time, Gibb had been decorated with two Distinguished Flying Crosses, four Air Medals and the Purple Heart.

Returning to the States, Gibb was released from the military on October 25, 1945. He reenlisted in the Air Force on October 10, 1947, and saw combat during the Korean War with the 8th Fighter-Bomber Group. He was killed on December 16, 1951, when his F-84 *Thunderjet* was shot down by anti-aircraft fire over Korea.

MYRON M. HNATIO
5 victories
Detroit

ON NOVEMBER 16,1920, Myron Mack Hnatio was born in Detroit, Michigan, the son of Dymtro and Mary Stelmech Hnatio. Myron answered his nation's call to service early in World War II, and was subsequently assigned to the Army Air Force's Aviation Cadet Program. On October 8, 1942, Hnatio was awarded his Army Air Force aviator's wings and the gold bars of a second lieutenant at Lake Charles, Louisiana. He was then shipped to the Pacific Theater of operations where he would see combat with the 5th Air Force's 348th Fighter Group. As a member of the 340th Fighter Squadron, Hnatio began flying missions in P-47 *Thunderbolts* out of New Guinea. Under the leadership of Col. Neel Kearby, the 348th Fighter Group was the only 5th Air Force unit equipped with the P-47. Though some officials were skeptical of the bulky fighter's value, Kearby and his men earned a reputation as one of the best fighting units in the Air Corps. The men of the 348th Fighter Group accounted for over 150 enemy aircraft destroyed in their first five months of combat, and produced some twenty aces during this time.

While serving his tour of duty in the Pacific, Hnatio participated in dozens of patrol and reconnaissance missions and provided escort to Allied bomber formations on many occasions. Five times he was credited with destruction of an enemy aircraft, the last of these kills coming on March 11, 1944. It was over the Japanese airfield of But, that Hnatio chased down a Mitsubishi *Zero*, and sprayed it with machine gun fire from dead astern. The enemy aircraft started smoking, rolled over and crashed into the sea. It was Hnatio's fifth kill, and he was an ace. For his skill, heroism, and achievement while serving in the Pacific, Hnatio was awarded three Distinguished Flying Crosses, five Air Medals and a Bronze Star, among others.

Following his return to the United States, Myron M. Hnatio elected to stay in the Air Force, and eventually retired at the rank of Lieutenant Colonel. He died on October 18, 2002 in Walkersville, Maryland, and was buried at Arlington National Cemetery.

DAVID P. PHILLIPS III
5 Victories
Kewadin

DAVID PATTERSON PHILLIPS III OF KEWADIN, was born on June 21, 1923 before attending the University of West Virginia. He enlisted in the Navy on September 25, 1942, and graduated from flight training in March of 1943. Following nearly two years of stateside duty, Phillips joined VF-30 flying F6F *Hellcats* from the decks of the USS *Belleau Wood*.

Scoring his first victory on April 6, 1945, Ensign Phillips's squadron ran into heavy aerial opposition on an afternoon fighter sweep over Okinawa. In a running dogfight that lasted nearly two hours, VF-30 was credited with a total of 47 kills with no losses. Phillips' contribution to the tally was one *Zeke* fighter and three "Val" dive bombers destroyed. Just six days later, Phillips again accounted for the destruction of a *Zeke,* this time shooting it down over the Pacific Ocean.

Now officially an ace, Phillips was sent back to the United States, and remained in the military after the war. He left active duty in 1947 to join the U.S. Steel Corporation, but continued to serve in the Navy Reserves, retiring as a Lieutenant in August of 1961. Today, Dave Phillips makes his home on Torch Lake in northern Michigan with his wife Mary. He is a recipient of the Silver Star, 2 Distinguished Flying Crosses, and 6 Air Medals.

ANDREW J. RITCHEY
5 victories
Flint

ANDREW JACKSON RITCHEY was born in Flint, Michigan on September 12, 1942. Joining the Army as an 18-year-old private on August 4, 1942, he later applied for flight training and entered aviation cadet training on February 6, 1943. Ritchey won his wings on February 6, 1944 and was subsequently assigned to the ninth Air Force's 354th Fighter Group stationed in France.

Flying the P-47 *Thunderbolt,* Ritchey accounted for his first kill, an FW-190 near Bittburg, Germany on Christmas Eve. Unfortunately, this victory was classified as only a probable due to the lack of a witness. Now flying a P-51 *Mustang,* Ritchey hit his stride in April of 1945, destroying three Focke-Wulf 190's over Erfurt Gotha on the third of the month. On April 14, he damaged an ME-262 jet, and rounded out his scoring on the 20th with two ME-109 kills.

Ritchey left the service as a Captain in January 1947, having been decorated with the Distinguished Service Cross, 2 Distinguished Flying Crosses, and 22 Air Medals. After a 10 month break from service, Ritchey rejoined the Air Force, later seeing additional combat over Korea. He retired from military service on October 22, 1967 at the rank of Colonel.

GERALD L. ROUNDS
5 Victories
Imlay City

GERALD LYNN ROUNDS was born on April 26, 1921 in Imlay City, Michigan. He joined the Army on July 22, 1940, and though trained as an aviation mechanic, requested training as a pilot. Accepted for the aviation cadet program, Rounds became one of very few enlisted pilots when he graduated from class 42-C at Kelly Field, Texas on March 7, 1942. By October, Rounds had received a commission as a Second Lieutenant, and had been assigned to the 82nd Fighter Group in Algeria.

Flying a P-38 *Lightning*, Rounds first shot down an enemy aircraft on February 6, 1943, when he downed an ME-109 near Gabes Airdrome. He logged his second kill on March 1, downing another '109 and was also credited with damaging two more ME-109's before the month was out. On May 24th, Rounds destroyed his third ME-109 and followed up with a fourth '109 kill on July 5, 1943. His final aerial victory was achieved on September 11, in an aerial dogfight between Priscotta and Agropoli.

After 82 combat missions, Lt. Rounds was rotated back to the United States where he served for the remainder of the war. He was released from the service on September 22, 1945, having been awarded the Distinguished Flying Cross with One Oak Leaf Cluster and the Air Medal with thirteen Oak Leaf Clusters.

Today, Gerry Rounds live in retirement near Cedar City, Utah.

MICHAEL T. RUSSO
5 victories
Bloomfield Hills

MICHAEL THOMAS RUSSO was born in Cleveland, Ohio on September 4, 1920. He was attending the University of Ohio on December 7, 1941 when he first learned that Pearl Harbor had been attacked, and immediately enlisted in the U.S. Army Air Force with a request to be assigned to pilot training. After receiving his primary flight school at Pine Bluff, Arkansas, Mike went through basic flight training, and went on to graduate from the Aviation Cadet Program at Moore Field near Mission, Texas in February of 1943. After arriving in Meridian, Mississippi to undergo pre-combat training, Russo was checked out in the bird he would soon fly into combat - The A-36 *Invader*. Basically a P-51A converted to accommodate dive bombing techniques in combat, the A-36's under-powered Alison engine made it a less than desirable aircraft to fly.

With only sixteen hours of flight time in the A-36, Mike received orders to report to the 27th Fighter-Bomber Group in North Africa in April of 1943. Russo's first aerial victory occurred on September 13, 1943, when as part of an eight-plane formation, Lt. Russo and his fellow Americans dove on twelve German FW-190's that had been strafing Allied shipping off the coast of Italy. In the melee that resulted, four Nazi fighters were destroyed, with Russo claiming one of them. Russo's next appointment with the squadron scoreboard came one month later in October. While strafing a JU-88 parked on a runway in the Rome area, Russo and his pals were bounced by seven ME-109's. Three of the Messerschmitts would be shot down by pilots of the 27th Fighter Group, with no losses on the American side. Russo did not get any, but on a second mission over the same area that day, he spotted a small Nazi biplane that had wandered into the area, and promptly shot in down in flames.

December 1943 proved to be a busy time for Russo. On the eighth day of the month, his flight of twelve A-36's was ordered to strafe Aversano Airfield in northern Italy. He caught a JU-52 transport plane just as it was taking off from the field, and after a quick burst from his machine guns, the German tri-motor exploded in a ball of flame, thus giving Mike Russo his third kill. Not long after attaining his JU-52 victory, Russo was directed to strafe a column of German troops on a road in northern Italy. Attacking with devastating results, Russo single-handedly halted their advance, inflicting a large amount of casualties to the enemy. Russo's crew chief surprised the young pilot when he painted the nickname "Killer Russo" on the tail of his A-36. Uncomfortable with the crew chief's choice of words, Mike soon removed the writing from his aircraft.

On December 30, 1943, Lt. Russo was leading a flight of twelve A-36's near Rome, when they were jumped by sixteen ME-109's. In the ensuing dogfight, Russo quickly shot down one of the attackers, and watched as it exploded in mid air. Turning his attention to another ME-109, he fired a burst in its direction, and saw this one plunge straight into the ground. These two kills, the last of Russo's career, made him a full-fledged Fighter Ace, and the only A-36 Ace in history.

Russo returned to the United States not long after this mission, and as a holder of the Silver Star with one oak leaf cluster, the Distinguished Flying Cross with one oak leaf cluster, and the Air Medal with fourteen oak leaf clusters, he participated in a large number of war bond drives. Russo received a promotion to Captain in 1944, but left service in the Army Air Force before the war came to an end. Following World War II, Mike Russo established a very successful business, MR Products, Inc., in Troy, Michigan. Mr. Russo, who now lives in Bloomfield Hills, Michigan holds a number of patents for his numerous inventions. Most prominent is that for "Mr. Chain," a plastic chain used for crowd control worldwide.

PETER J. VAN DER LINDEN, JR.
5 Victories
Ironwood

PETER JOSEPH VAN DER LINDEN, JR. was born on July, 16, 1920 in Ironwood, Michigan and attended Purdue University prior to his enlistment in the Navy on May 18, 1942. Completing his training as a Navy pilot, Van Der Linden was assigned to VF-8 flying F6F *Hellcat* fighters onboard the USS *Bunker Hill* against the Japanese.

Ensign Van Der Linden got his first taste of aerial combat on March 30, 1944, when he was credited with probably destroying a *Zeke* fighter between Peleliu and Augaur Islands. On September 21, Van Der Linden Shot down a "Tony" fighter over Clark Field to chalk up his first confirmed kill. October 12th saw him participate in an early morning fighter sweep over Formosa, and it was during this mission that his squadron encountered heavy resistance from a swarm of Japanese fighters. In the swirling dogfight that resulted, Van Der Linden was credited with three enemy aircraft destroyed. He went on to make ace just two days later with a "Kate" bomber shot up over the Pacific to end his scoring.

In 1945, Van Der Linden joined VF-94 and served on the USS *Lexington* until the end of the war. Staying in the Navy, Van Der Linden was promoted to the rank of Lieutenant Commander on August 1, 1955 and left the service in 1958. Now living in Joliet, Illinois, Lt.

Commander Van Der Linden is a recipient of two Distinguished Flying Crosses and four Air Medals.

LEE V. WISEMAN
Grand Rapids
5 victories

LEE VERN WISEMAN, a native of Grand Rapids, Michigan, was born on March 29, 1921. He graduated from high school in 1939 and enlisted in the Army Air Corps in August of 1940. Wiseman was sent to flight training in December of 1941, and graduated with class 42-G on August 5, 1942. He checked out in P-38's on the west coast before being shipped out to North Africa in October of 1942, where he was assigned to the 7th Fighter Squadron of the 1st Fighter Group. Wiseman would fly his first combat missions in January of 1943. In February of that year, he scored his first kill, an FW-190, while participating in a B-17 escort mission. He claimed three more kills, 2 Ju-52' s and an Italian Macchi 202 in April, and rounded out his scoring with another FW-190 he bagged on a fighter sweep over the Gulf of Tunis. During this time, Wiseman had risen to the rank of Major, with command of the 7th Fighter Squadron. By the end of the war, he had received the Silver Star, Legion of Merit with one Oak Leaf Cluster, the Distinguished Flying Cross with one Oak Leaf Cluster, and the Air Medal with 12 oak leave clusters.

Following his service in World War II, Wiseman spent many years in the field of Air Force Logistics, commanding several units within the Strategic Air Command Structure. He eventually retired from military service with the rank of Colonel.

MICHAEL R. YUNCK
5 Victories
Detroit

MICHAEL RYAN YUNCK was born on August 19, 1918 in Detroit. He attended the University of Michigan for one year before switching to the US Naval Academy in Annapolis, Maryland. Commissioned as a Marine Corps 2nd Lieutenant in November of 1941, Yunck was assigned to VMO-251, based on Guadalcanal. He flew his F4F *Wildcat* in operations against the Japanese, and was shot down on one occasion by enemy ground fire. Fortunately, he was rescued by friendly natives who returned him to his squadron two weeks later.

On December 3, 1942, Yunck was credited with downing three enemy float planes near New Georgia Island to open his account. However, he was soon rotated home for a rest tour, and later was reassigned as commander of VMF-311. Flying an F4U *Corsair*, Yunck returned to combat in the Pacific and shot down two Zeke fighters on July 2nd, 1945 to become one of the last Marine Corps aces of World War II.

After the Japanese surrender in August of 1945, Yunck returned to the States where he served as a test pilot. He again saw combat during the Korean War, this time as logistics officer for Marine Air Group 33. In 1963, Yunck was designated "Marine Aviator of the Year" and was presented with the Alfred A. Cunningham trophy. When the Vietnam War erupted in the late 1960's Yunck was again sent into combat, serving as operations officer for the 1st Marine Air Wing. While flying as a helicopter co pilot on December 10, 1965, Yunck was shot down south of Danang. Critically wounded, it was decided that his right leg would have to amputated, which forced him to retire at the rank of Colonel after many years of faithful service. A recipient of two Silver Stars, the Distinguished Flying Cross, a Bronze Star, two Air Medals, and the Purple Heart, Michael R. Yunck passed away on September 28, 1984 in Solvang, California after a long battle with cancer.

THE KOREAN WAR 1950-1953

CECIL G. FOSTER
9 victories
Midland

A NATIVE OF MIDLAND, Cecil Glenn Foster was born on the 30th of August, 1925. He grew up on a 10-acre farm in Midland County, and had his first look at an airplane when his father took him over to see a Ford Tri Motor that had landed near their farm. They couldn't afford a ride, but young Cecil enjoyed it anyway. When he was five, Cecil's mother died of polio. This made life very difficult for the Fosters, and Cecil was then cared for by his Grandparents. He went on to graduate from Midland High School in 1943, and soon afterward enlisted in the Army Air Force in Battle Creek, Michigan.

After completing his training as a B-24 navigator, Foster was commissioned as a Second Lieutenant at San Marcos, Texas on February 10, 1945. He then served various stateside duties until the end of World War II, and was later transferred to Grand Island Army Air Base in Nebraska. It was here that Lt. Foster requested appointment to the Air Force Flight Training Program. He entered flight school at Randolph Air Field, Texas in January of 1947, and graduated as a fighter pilot in February, 1948. After serving as a flight instructor at Hensley Field, Texas, Foster was released from service in the Air Force.

In August 1951, Foster was recalled to active duty for the Korean War. He was assigned to the 16th Fighter

Squadron, 51st Fighter Interceptor Wing, and arrived in Korea on May 30, 1952. He immediately began flying combat missions, shooting down his first MiG on September 7,1952. He scored again on September 26, and downed his fourth Chinese jet on October 16. Foster gained his fifth kill, and his status as an ace on November 22, when he shot down another MiG-15 over the Yalu River. Cecil downed his sixth jet on January 6, 1953, and his seventh on the 22nd of that month. Two days later, Foster rounded out his scoring with two MiG-15's destroyed on his 100th and final mission of the Korean War. His tally would stand at 9 confirmed and 2 damaged, making Foster the 24th jet ace in history, ranked with the 12th highest score on the list of Korean War aces.

After returning from Korea, Foster decided to make the Air Force a career. During the Vietnam War, he assumed command of the 390th Tactical Fighter Squadron stationed at DaNang, Air Force Base and subsequently logged an additional 168 combat missions in F-4 Phantom jets. Colonel Foster retired from the military on July 1, 1975, ending a distinguished military career that very few have ever matched. Now living in Henderson, Nevada, Colonel Foster is a holder of the Silver Star with one oak leaf cluster, the Distinguished Flying Cross with two oak leaf clusters, the Bronze Star, the Purple Heart, the Air Medal with 12 oak leaf clusters, and Vietnam's Gallantry Cross medal with one Gold Star.

WINTON W. "BONES" MARSHALL
6.5 victories
Detroit

WINTON WHITTIER MARSHALL was born in 1919 in Detroit, Michigan before beginning his military career in 1942 at the age of 23. He earned his wings of silver at Yuma Army Air Base, Arizona and was commissioned a Second Lieutenant in April of 1943. His first military assignment was with the 326th Fighter Gunnery Training Group stationed at Las Vegas Army Air Field in Nevada. Marshall was soon named chief of the base's P-39 Training Section; a position he held until February, 1945, when he was sent to the Panama Canal Zone as a pilot with the 36th Fighter Group. Marshall's post- WWII assignments included a stint as operations officer of the 48th Fighter Squadron, which then part of the 14th Fighter Group. Based at Dow Field, Maine, this unit had the distinction of being the first squadron to fly the F-84 *Thunderjet*, and soon Marshall was one of the most proficient F-84 pilots in the world.

In 1950, the United States was caught up in a new war in a far-off land called Korea. When the United States asked Marshall to lead the 335th Fighter Squadron which based in the heart of South Korea, he gladly accepted. As part of the 4th Fighter Wing, the 335th was equipped with F-86 *Sabres*, and would soon gain a reputation as one of the top units of the Korean Conflict. Marshall got onto the scoreboard early in his combat tour with a MiG destroyed on September 2, 1951. By no means an easy kill, Bones wrestled with this MiG-15 fighter for nearly half an hour before shooting him down in flames somewhere between Sinuju, and Puongsong, South Korea. He was awarded his well-deserved first air victory upon his return to Kimpo airfield later that day. Marshall would not claim another kill until November 28, 1951, when he downed two MiG-15's over the Yalu River. He followed up with two more kills on the 30th to become the fifth Jet Ace of the Korean War. By the end of his Korean War combat tour in January, 1952, Marshall's score had reached 6.5 confirmed victories, seven probably destroyed, and six damaged.

In the years following the Korean War, Marshall served in various capacities in the United States and abroad, most notably as Deputy Director of Operations for the Joint Chiefs of Staff. He was sent to South West Asia during the Vietnam War with an appointment as Vice Commander, Seventh Air Force, and went on to serve as Vice Commander in Chief, Pacific Air Forces before returning to the United States in June of 1975. He then served as Deputy Commander in Chief, U.S. Readiness Command at MacDill Air Force Base, Florida. He retired from the Air Force as a Lieutenant General on September 1, 1977, having served his country faithfully for over 35 years. General Marshall is a recipient of two Distinguished Service Medals, the Silver Star, four Legions of Merit, three Distinguished Flying Crosses, the Bronze Star, six Air Medals, and the Purple Heart. He now lives with his wife, Millie in Honolulu, Hawaii.

IVEN C. KINCHELOE, JR.
5 victories
Cassopolis

IVEN CARL KINCHELOE, JR. was a pilot's pilot. Born in Detroit on July 2, 1928, he and his family moved to Cassopolis when he was three. From the very beginning, he knew what he wanted to do with his life. As a teenager, Kincheloe began saving his hard-earned money to pay for flying lessons, and by age 14 he had accumulated enough hours to fly solo, though the law required him to wait until he was sixteen. For two years he waited, flying every chance got. By the time he finally earned his pilot's license on his sixteenth birthday, Iven had logged over 200 flight hours, more than many of his instructors had.

Kincheloe graduated from the ROTC program in 1948 and was commissioned as a Second Lieutenant in the Air Force Reserve. After completing his flight training at Perrin Air Force Base, Texas, Kincheloe received his silver pilot's wings on August 4, 1950. With the Korean War now under way, it would not be long before Kincheloe was in combat. After undergoing various checks and tests in the F-86 *Sabre*, Kincheloe arrived in Korea in September of 1951. He was assigned to the 325th Fighter Interceptor Squadron as a replacement pilot, and was soon flying escort missions for B-29's. After completing sixteen combat missions with the 325th, Iven was transferred to the 25th Fighter Squadron of the 51st Fighter Interceptor Wing, based at Suwan, Korea.

January 25, 1952 was a memorable day for Lt. Kincheloe. While on a combat mission over enemy territory, one of the pilots in his flight spotted three bandits flying at low altitude over the hills of Korea. The four Americans dove on the unsuspecting MiG's and took them completely by surprise. Kincheloe latched onto the tail of the first MiG, and let a burst go from his six fifty-caliber machine guns. With a huge explosion, the communist fighter blew up in his face, giving Kincheloe his first confirmed victory.

A week later, Kincheloe received a promotion to Captain, and shot down another MiG. His next successes came on April 1, 1952, his best day in combat, when he claimed two MiG-15's destroyed. Just a few days later he was involved in an escort mission over enemy territory, and had the opportunity to down another MiG as it was making a run on the bombers. It his Kincheloe's fifth kill, which gave him credit as being the 10th pilot to make ace during the Korean War. When Kincheloe's tour of duty ended in the middle of May, 1952, he had flown one hundred and thirty-one combat missions, which included one hundred and one in F-86's, and thirty in F-80's. His aerial combat record stood at five confirmed, eleven damaged, and five destroyed on the ground.

Though Iven Kincheloe's contributions to the Korean War effort are undeniable, he is best remembered for his services as a test pilot in the late 1950's. His most notable feat came while flying the X-2 experimental aircraft on September 7, 1956, when he become the first human ever to enter into space. For his contributions to the advancement of space exploration, Kincheloe received the Mackay Trophy for completing the most meritorious flight of 1956 – not to mention the nickname "First of the Spacemen."

Though his life was cut short by a tragic aircraft accident on July 26, 1958, Kincheloe's service to his country was honored on September 25, 1959, with the dedication of Kincheloe Air Force Base in Kinross, Michigan. The base was a key site in the Strategic Air Command structure until its closure in 1977.

EPILOGUE

THESE ARE THE STORIES OF MICHIGAN'S FIGHTER ACES; fifty-six men who distinguished themselves by earning a place in history as some of the finest military aviators the world has ever known. Men of action, men of courage, and most of all men of patriotism, these individuals played a key role in both the development of aviation and in the defense of our freedoms during every war of the 20th Century.

Though the era of the fighter ace will eventually pass away from us entirely, we can be thankful that the things these men fought for will never die. Things like freedom, liberty, and justice will live for ever thanks in part to the sacrifices these individuals once made for us.

Though time moves forward and our world constantly changes, a perpetual responsibility has been left to us: to remember those veterans who fought on our behalf, and to ensure that their sacrifices were not in vain.

APPENDIX
Complete List of Michigan's Fighter Aces
(All made ace in World War II unless noted)

1. Mahurin, Walker M. - 24.5 (Ann Arbor)
2. Kepford, Ira C. – 17 (Muskegon)
3. DeLong, Phillip C. - 13.17 (Jackson)
4. Rigg, James Francis – 11 (Saginaw)
5. Fiebelkorn, Ernest C. - 9.5 (Lake Orion)
6. Foster, Cecil G. – 9 (Midland) (Korea)
7. Wolfe, Judge Edmond – 9 (Flint)
8. Bryan, William E., Jr. - 8.5 (Flint)
9. Foster, Carl Clifford - 8.5 (Detroit)
10. Plant, Claude W. - 8.5 (Grand Rapids)
11. Hadden, Mayo A., Jr. – 8 (Holland)
12. Hilton, D'Arcy F. – 8 (Detroit) (WWI)
13. Novotny, George P. – 8 (Allen Park)
14. Weaver, Charles E. - 8 (Detroit)
15. Morris, James M. - 7.3 (Detroit)
16. Lombard, John D. – 7 (Ionia)
17. Purdy, John E. – 7 (Wyandotte)
18. Tyler, Gerald E. – 7 (Hart)
19. Waters, Edward T. -7 (Highland Park)
20. Wesoloski, John M. – 7 (Detroit)
21. Marshall, Winton W. - 6.5 (Detroit) (Korea)
22. Davenport, Merl W. - 6.25 (Sterling Heights)
23. Conant, Arthur R. - 6 (Crystal Lake)
24. Drew, Urban L. - 6 (Detroit)
25. Edinger, Charles E. – 6 (Onaway)
26. Larson, Leland A. - 6 (Whitemore)
27. Mugavero, James D. – 6 (Port Huron)

28. Pond, Zenneth A. – 6 (Hillsdale Co.)
29. Rounds, Gerald L. - 6 (Imlay City)
30. Visscher, Herman W. - 6 (Portage)
31. Welch, Robert E. - 6 (Brown City)
32. Winfield, Murray - 6 (Detroit)
33. Koraleski, Walter J. - 5.53 (Detroit)
34. Hood, William L. - 5.5 (Kalamazoo)
35. Maas, John B. 5.5 (Lansing)
36. McPharlin, Michael G.H. - 5.5 (Hastings)
37. Smith, Donovan F. - 5.5 (Dowagiac)
38. Wood, Walter A. - 5.5 (Ionia)
39. Prichard, Melvin M. - 5.25 (Gaylord)
40. Baldwin, Frank B. – 5 (Flint)
41. Bank, Raymond M. – 5 (Kendall)
42. Barkey, Robert M. – 5 (Wyandotte)
43. Carlton, William A. – 5 (Saginaw)
44. Duffy, Richard E. – 5 (Walled Lake)
45. Fair, John W. – 5 (Battle Creek)
46. Gibb, Robert D. – 5 (Detroit)
47. Grange, Edward R. – 5 (Lansing) (WWI)
48. Hnatio, Myron M. – 5 (Detroit)
49. Kincheloe, Iven C. – 5 (Cassopolis) (Korea)
50. Philips, David P. III - 5 (Kewadin)
51. Porter, Ken L. - 5 (Dowagiac) (WWI)
52. Ritchie, Andrew J. - 5 (Flint)
53. Russo, Michael T. – 5 (Troy)
54. Van Der Linden, Peter J. – 5 (Ironwood)
55. Wiseman, Lee Vern - 5 (Grand Rapids)
56. Yunck, Michael R. - 5 (Detroit)

BIBLIOGRAPHY

Boyce, J. Ward. *The American Fighter Aces Album.* American Fighter Aces Association, 1996.

Cora, Paul B. *Yellowjackets: The 361st Fighter Group in World War II.* Schiffer Military Publishing, 2002

Foster, Cecil G. *MiG Alley to MuGhia Pass.* McFarland and Company Publishers. 2001.

Goebel, Robert J. *Mustang Ace.* Pacifica Press, 1991.

Hess, William. *America's Top WWII Aces in Their Own Words.* MBI Publishing Company 2001

Miller, Thomas G. *The Cactus Air Force.* Harper and Row, 1969

Morris, Danny. *Aces and Wingmen II, Vol. 1.* Aviation Usk, 1989.

Powell, R.R. and Drew, U. L. *Ben Drew – The Katzenjammer Ace.* Drew Enterprises, 1998.

Tillman, Barrett. *US Navy Fighters of WWII.* MBI Publishing Company 1998.

Toliver, Raymond F. *Fighter Aces of the USA.* Schiffer Military Publishing 1997.

Various Authors. *Osprey Aircraft of the Aces Series.* Osprey Publishing.

ABOUT THE AUTHOR

A NATIVE OF BATTLE CREEK, MICHIGAN, Andrew Layton has enjoyed a love for history ever since he can remember. Having studied the lives of American Fighter Aces since the age of 12, he has amassed one of the largest collections of ace-related memorabilia in the world. Layton, who attends South Side Bible Church in Battle Creek, frequently volunteers in his community and is active in the VA's *Stories of Service* project, having been recognized by congress for his contributions in this area. He is also an associate member of the American Fighter Aces Association and frequently lectures on various historical topics. This is his first book.

Printed in the United States
29112LVS00001B/421-438